EXTRAORDINARY
LIVES

MEMBERS SINCE 1958

FOREWORD BY SUSAN ORLEAN

Library of Congress Cataloging-in-Publication Data
Library of Congress Control Number: 2008937962

Produced and published by
American Express Company
New York, New York

Managing Editor Peg Tyre
Cover illustration by Si Scott
Biography portraits by Alexandra Compain-Tissier
Design by VSA Partners, Inc., New York
Printing by Blanchette Press

First Edition

CONTENTS

TO OUR CARDMEMBERS SINCE 1958

This is a book of extraordinary stories: tales of courage, of compassion, of character. Stories about the pursuit of dreams and the joy of creative expression, about perseverance and service to others. Stories of abiding loyalty—to family and friends, to deeply held values, to community, to country. Above all, they are stories about lives exceedingly well lived. They are your stories.

In 1958, we introduced the American Express Card. It helped bring about a revolution in the way people paid for goods and services the world over, and it changed our company forever. We thought the most fitting way to honor this milestone would be to pay tribute to those Cardmembers who have been with us from the beginning. After all, it is you—our earliest adopters—who launched the Card's 50-year success story.

As Susan Orlean so eloquently notes in her foreword on the following pages, our charter members are a truly remarkable group. While we cannot tell all of your stories here, we believe this collection reflects the panorama of your individual accomplishments, as well as some of the life experiences you share. The stories inside are told by some of the finest writers and illustrators practicing their art today.

To all of our Cardmembers since 1958, this is our gift to you. Your inspiring life stories represent the best of the human spirit. It has been our privilege to serve you for 50 years, and we look forward to many more.

SINCERELY,

Ken Chenault

KEN CHENAULT
Chairman and CEO, American Express Company

FOREWORD

Some people just know how to live. They build, they join, they persevere, they progress. They start from nothing and make something. They start with something and do new things with it. They establish companies and families and communities and clubs. When they have setbacks, they see them as good stories; when they experience defeat, they treat it as the start of a new chapter. They do grand things, and they do modest things, but they do all of it with the same steady certainty that what comes next will be even better than what came before.

There is no social group that has a monopoly on this talent for living, but there is a noticeable concentration of it in the generation born in the early years of the 20th century, and particularly, it seems, among the people who decided, in 1958, to join up with this new notion of a charge card offered by American Express. Charge cards were not a common item back then, and signing up for one was a bit of a gamble. The decision to try something a little out of the ordinary was not unusual for this group of people; in fact, it was a logical expression of the core of their nature — their spirit of enterprise, their great curiosity, their strong ambition and their willingness to embrace something new if it offered possibility and promise.

Over the last few months, American Express has come to know many of these charter members even better through their stories. In connection with the Card's 50th anniversary, they were asked a few questions — what they've done professionally, what they're proud of, what they've overcome, what they do each day — and what they sent in response were marvelous anecdotes and quick sketches of lives that have been wonderfully varied and deeply felt. What is most striking is that the stories they chose to tell are not simply stories of success: They are also tales of accomplishment against the odds, of rebound and endurance. And even though the charter members are, by and large, people who have done well for themselves, the achievements they celebrate with the greatest pride are not material ones; they are appreciations of family, health, experience, wisdom and happiness. Meeting this group of people makes you realize that what they know about living isn't merely how to enjoy good things, but, more important, how to find what is truly good in life.

Their professions and experiences and backgrounds are as wide as the world. Doctors, lawyers, pilots, professors; butchers, bakers, candlestick makers; inventors, artists, business founders; people who did one thing their whole life long and others who changed professions several times. Men and women. Native-born and immigrants. Coming from money and coming from nothing. Educated, self-taught, instant successes and steady toilers. Their commonality is more a matter of character than of demographics. They are, above all and most definitively, optimists.

What accounts for their buoyancy? It can't be attributed to the sweetness of the period into which they were born—for most charter members, their childhood unfolded when the country was still bruised and aching in the aftermath of the First World War. Some fizzy years followed, of course, but these folks crossed into adolescence and young adulthood with what was unfortunate timing. Whatever might have been carefree was tamped down, hard, by the Great Depression; their first legacy was those sour times. When asked what their biggest challenges in life had been, many talked about the Depression and just how deep it cut:

> *"[I was] blown from here to there in dust storms with limited family support."*

> *"[I was] from a poor immigrant family and lived through the Depression."*

> *"My penniless status from 1940 to 1943."*

> *"Being born into a proud but poor, working-class family in the Great Depression in 1931."*

In some cases, childhood was abbreviated not just by economics but by family circumstances as well.

> *"[I was responsible] for raising three siblings at age 14,"* wrote one charter member.

And another:

> *"I had to overcome the doubts and trepidations that came with losing my father at age 11 and starting to work full-time at age 13."*

> *"I was the youngest child of immigrants from Poland and the Ukraine . . . and was orphaned before I was 10."*

> *"My father died when I was 13, and my mother died four years later. With no living grandparents, I became the family breadwinner for two brothers and a sister. . . ."*

It is tempting to assume that the meanness of the Depression and the burden of taking on so many adult responsibilities at a young age would have depleted them, but it instead nurtured a resilience that they turned to again and again. That was especially fortunate, since the next trial that life presented to this generation was even more grueling. In 1939, Hitler invaded Poland, and the brittle peace in Europe cracked apart. Two years later, the United States was in the war, and everything changed—and these were the people who were most changed by it. They fought in the war and were surprised to survive it. They were battered by it ("As a result of 'ditching' in an army passenger airplane, 18 of 26 aboard were killed; I suffered severe injuries"). They lost family ("My brother was killed in the first wave at Normandy") and, in some cases, their futures ("I was married at 18 and a month later, he was killed in WWII"). But the pain was shot through with pride. And what's more, it was a dramatic introduction to the power of shared purpose. As Mary Lou Chapman, a Red Cross stalwart and charter member, says, "*Everybody* was doing something to help the war effort then." The war years, for all their hardships, also provided an object lesson in the benefits of joining forces, and the lesson took. Perhaps no other generation has put more value on the social capital that grows out of community and connection, and savored the memberships that in many cases defined their lives.

The year 1958 started with a thump. Early that January, Sputnik, which had been orbiting the earth for three months, wore out its batteries and came tumbling back through the atmosphere. It was a tidy symbol of the time, capturing the new aspirations (space and technology), the prevailing politics (the United States' rivalry with the Soviet Union) and the pace of innovation that had picked up dramatically in the aftermath of the war, bringing some spectacular advances and the occasional thud.

This was the year that signaled the end to the baby boom, the end of the Packard, the end of the Brooklyn Dodgers (who became the Los Angeles Dodgers that summer), the end to a wartime navy (the USS *Wisconsin* was decommissioned in March—the first time since 1895 that the United States didn't have an active battleship). The war was over, of course, but it was still present in smaller ways. Elvis Presley's induction into the army in 1958 made international news; more sobering was the first burial of World War II and Korean War soldiers at the Tomb of the Unknowns in Arlington Cemetery. The world was a much smaller place then—a population of slightly under 3 billion, compared to close to 7 billion today—and while it was no longer convulsed in battle, it was still unsettled. Mao began the Great Leap Forward in China; Fidel Castro began broadcasting from his rebel radio station in the mountains of Cuba; Khrushchev, the new head of the Soviet Union, lurched between progressive reform and totalitarian ruthlessness;

Vice President Richard Nixon, on a tour of Latin America, was met with jeering, protesting crowds.

Everything was in flux, but many of the changes in the United States were auspicious. We established NASA and saw the first Pan Am Clipper jet service from New York to Paris. We met, for the first time, Alvin and the Chipmunks, the hula hoop, cardiac pacemakers, the Monterey Jazz Festival and Nabokov's *Lolita*. The ugliness of segregation still hung over the country, but in 1958, the first African-American flight attendant was hired and the first African-American student graduated from Arkansas' previously all-white Little Rock Central High School. Harry Winston donated the Hope Diamond to the Smithsonian. Pope Pius XII declared Saint Clare the patron saint of television. The peace symbol was designed.

The American economy was pitching up and down during that period; 1958, in fact, began in a recession. Hardly a moment to launch a new financial product, you might think, except that it was the moment when the people of this generation, toughened by the Depression and fortified by the experience of living through the war, were coming into their own as entrepreneurs and professionals. Recession notwithstanding, they were busily building a new economy in this country, and a new identity for themselves as the modern American business class. One early American Express advertisement suggested the Card would suit you "if you appreciate the practical value and prestige of credit." Evidently, thousands of people did appreciate value and prestige, and considered themselves, as the ad further suggested, "progressive," and they requested the Card in numbers far beyond what American Express expected. The company had hoped for 400,000 members by the end of four years. Instead, they had 500,000 by the end of three months. Besides its usefulness for credit and accounting, the Card—initially, just a piece of purple-tinted paper—signified something much deeper. Decades before the notion of globalization became commonplace, the American Express Card recognized that American business was no longer based in the corner shop and the local market, but was becoming a far-flung and flourishing network, and a charge card was a natural accessory to society's new fluidity and mobility. And it signified something on a more personal level: Becoming a member of American Express meant really joining something, rather than just acquiring a convenience. It meant making a connection with a distinct group of people in this country who had emerged from those hard times energized and determined, who wanted to make things happen, who were forward-thinking and effective. While they knew firsthand the importance of the individual, they also enjoyed the sense of being part of something bigger than themselves.

And they certainly did make things happen. They struck out in every direction imaginable, building careers and companies, and making the next 50 years this country's most vibrant period. It is as if the world as we know it today was set in motion then, in the mid-1950s, by this generation's achievement.

"[Working for the space program,] I helped choose the first group of astronauts."

"I developed intraocular lenses to help post-cataract patients."

"I was one of the first female FBI employees."

"I started an airline when all of the established ones were going out of business."

"I succeeded in a broadcasting career after the sudden death of my husband when I was 40 years old."

"I helped design textiles, aerospace valves, timers, medical equipment."

"I was the first chairman of the largest economic development organization in the world."

"I provided architectural services to people, helping them build the homes they wanted."

"I conceived and manufactured the fertilizer which became the most-used phosphate fertilizer in the world."

"I had a large family medical practice for 50 years."

"I helped changed the face of professional baseball photography."

"I was a judge."

"I taught."

They marched through the next five decades with the same intrepidness that had buoyed them during the Depression and World War II, raising families, spreading out across the country, making the world work. There were certainly impediments along the way. They had businesses rise spectacularly and then, sometimes, fall—many charter members mentioned having gone through more than one cycle of success and failure. But each time they picked up and started anew. They lost spouses to illness but managed to find happiness again; they were tested by a society just learning to expand its embrace ("Being black, a woman and relatively young…I had to prove my capabilities") and tested again ("In 2001, at age 80, the stock market collapsed and I lost most of my life's savings. Undaunted, I developed a new product….") and continued on without bitterness and with a fresh dose of ingenuity. And they did very well for themselves. But rather than viewing success and comfort as their entitlement after going through hard times, the generation that these charter members are part of seemed to renew regularly the feeling that they in fact have been lucky in life. "I have never had a bad day," one cardmember wrote. As they came into their own as parents and professionals, their appreciation for their run of good days grew into a great generosity, making this probably the most philanthropic, civic-minded and family-minded of any generation this country has ever known. They ended up giving back much more than many of them probably ever dreamed that they would have.

In 1958, when the American Express Card debuted, my father, Arthur Orlean, was 43 years old. He had been born during World War I, served in World War II, struggled in the Depression. His father—my grandfather Sam—had deserted the czar's army in Russia around the turn of the century and made his way, hat in hand, to America. Working as a carpenter and then, on a modest scale, as a developer, Sam made a barely middle-class life for my grandmother and their four children. My father was 14 when the stock market crashed, and he watched my grandfather lose his buildings one by one and, along with them, his hopefulness. At that point in his life, my dad knew how to do very little other than roller-skate and shoot marbles, but like so many of his friends, he went to work doing whatever he could to help muddle through those years. The pounding my grandfather took in the Depression left him wary and disillusioned. The effect on my dad was nearly the opposite: He took it as a mighty challenge. He put himself through college and, after his years in the army, eked out enough working odd jobs to put himself through law school. Despite having witnessed the quicksilver of my grandfather's real estate dreams, my father decided, a few years out of law school, to develop buildings on his own. He built a few, made good on the deal, built a few more. By 1958, he had a solid business, a score of employees and a feeling of accomplishment that gave him the kind of satisfaction that only something a little surprising can impart. My father loved innovation and liked getting a head start on anything promising, so he signed up for the American Express Card as soon as it was announced. I was only three years old in 1958, so I have no independent memory of the day the purple paper card arrived at our house, but I can imagine that my father was incredibly proud of being a charter member and quick to put it to use. One of my most vivid early memories was the delight I had in watching him, time and time again, open his wallet and pull out that card, and suddenly almost anything was possible. It made him seem invincible.

My father had a lot in his life—a nice house, a great car, a terrific wife and three grateful kids, many good friends, standing in his community, a thriving business—and he never took any of it for granted, ever. It was clear to me that this little card, with his name embossed across the bottom, symbolized quite a lot more to him than a way to pay bills. It marked his passage, via hard work and hope, into adulthood, prosperity and confidence. He carried that card every day—from the moment he got it in 1958 until he passed away last year. It was in his wallet almost exactly 50 years, and he never stopped appreciating what it said about how he had lived his life.

So these are my heroes, those of you who, like my dad, midwifed the world we live in now, sometimes with great, sweeping gestures and often with countless smaller, specific ones; famous around the world or perhaps just famous in your own backyard; most of all, enduringly upbeat, moving forward with a bright, brisk optimism regardless of the times. You knew, most of all, how to hold on to what was dear, what mattered, what would last, and that's the greatest accomplishment here—that for these last 50 years you've made the world spin a little faster without ever letting the important things go.

SINCERELY,

SUSAN ORLEAN

On Guard

by JUDY BACHRACH

illustrations by TAVIS COBURN

T IS ONLY FITTING THAT NICHOLAS BELTRANTE DECIDES TO RECOUNT the remarkable details of his event-packed life on June 17, 2008—and not simply because that date happens to be the former detective's 81st birthday. Back in 1972, June 17 was also the day of the Watergate break-in at the Democratic National Committee headquarters, an incident that ensnared not only the five burglars who were discovered attempting to bug the place, but also then-President Richard M. Nixon, who first tried to cover up the scandal, and subsequently had to resign.

Unsurprisingly to those who know him, ace private eye Nick Beltrante was hired two days after the burglars were caught in the act. His mission: to debug the Watergate offices and uncover who among the many volunteers ostensibly helping out Democratic presidential candidate George McGovern might have been secretly working for Nixon's people. That was par for the course for Beltrante. Throughout his career, first as a Washington, D.C., cop and then as a private eye heading his own investigative firm, Beltrante usually managed to be where the action was. As a policeman, he arrived on the scene minutes after one presidential assassination attempt, and stayed close to three presidents in order to foil others. It was perhaps inevitable that as a private eye he was sent in to sort out the political disaster that became known simply as Watergate.

Working for the Democratic National Committee, Beltrante supervised the dismantling of hundreds of campaign office phones in order to check for hidden microphones and transmitters. This process went on for weeks, every night, 10 p.m. to 6 a.m. "We never found any bugs implanted in the Watergate phones," Beltrante says, patently disappointed. However, certain McGovern volunteers, he informed the Democratic presidential candidate, were very likely moles, and needed to be dismissed. And the probing of another McGovern venue nearby revealed a lot more—although few aside from Beltrante and his clients knew this at the time.

"At the McGovern for President headquarters, we detected electronic vibrations in one of the walls—and on the opposite side of that wall there was an office building that had been rented to one of the Watergate perpetrators," Beltrante explains. "They were trying to electronically listen through the wall to what was being said in McGovern's office next door."

Washington, D.C., being the kind of place it is, Beltrante's counterespionage operation couldn't remain a complete secret for long. "I had many, many visits from

Carl Bernstein and Bob Woodward in my office where we discussed the bugging," he says, referring to the *Washington Post* reporters whose investigative work on Watergate won their newspaper a Pulitzer Prize.

As for Beltrante, he got his own prizes: $5,000 and considerable renown for his efforts in rectifying the security weaknesses of the Democrats and fingering possible moles. ("The McGovern people were so damn careless, I couldn't believe it!" he confides.)

He also became the guardian of the famous thick-set gray Watergate safe, once the repository of checks and cash, as well as lists of generous contributors to the Democratic Party. That safe was Beltrante's last request of his clients, who were more than happy to rid themselves of the unwieldy item once McGovern lost the election. To this day, it sits in the crowded basement of the former detective's suburban Virginia house, shielding its own tempting store of secrets. "Oh, hell, I have things in there you'd love to see," Beltrante tells me.

"The dean of the private-eye corps in the nation's capital," as *Money* magazine once described him, is still sturdy-looking, with shrewd green eyes set in a broad, pensive face, and an old-fashioned sense of humor. Visitors, on their departure, are handed a $1 million bill stamped with Beltrante's old picture from his police days, when the plainclothes detective had red hair. He began his career first as a traffic cop, next as a cop on the beat, and finally as a police detective. At 23, he was not only the youngest one on the force but part of presidential security. This meant he was often assigned to assist the Secret Service in helping protect a series of commanders-in-chief. As a public servant,

he may not have seen everything, but he saw a heck of a lot. He had the uncanny knack of being anywhere anything exciting was happening.

It wasn't always this way. The son of an Italian immigrant father who worked on the Pennsylvania railroad and a mother also of Italian descent, Beltrante grew up in Atlantic City, New Jersey ("A wonderful city!"), with dreams of becoming a pharmacist. At 17, during World War II, he signed up with the navy and was assigned to the hospital ship *Consolation* as a pharmacist mate. After a year and a half, he joined the United States Marine Corps Reserve for four years.

When he returned home, however, law enforcement seemed like it would be a more exciting—and lucrative—career. In 1949, for example, Washington, D.C.'s Metropolitan police force was offering new recruits $3,077 a year. "Nice pay for the era," Beltrante recalls.

And for a while, that salary was his only source of satisfaction. Beltrante spent a few desultory months directing downtown traffic: "Visitors would come up to me and say, 'Where is 14th and G NW?' And I would say, 'I don't know, I'm new here!' Well, it was just one street up from where I was directing traffic," he recalls.

Far more rewarding was his next assignment: Beltrante patrolled the Georgetown area of Washington—an upscale neighborhood crammed with pretty Federal-style homes and small gardens where everyone who was anyone liked to live. He liked being close to power. For Beltrante on his new beat, the influential and the famous were not simply the substance of headlines or brief, flickering images on the television news. They were his community and he, their protector.

Supreme Court Justice Hugo Black used to greet Beltrante, as did General George C. Marshall (creator of the Marshall Plan), who used to walk his tiny dog with the young policeman by his side. The young John F. Kennedy also passed by. "I ignored him," says Beltrante, who thought the career of the ambitious junior senator from Massachusetts would essentially go nowhere.

Despite his flawed predictive powers regarding major historical events, the young cop nonetheless demonstrated early on an impressive ability to pop up wherever they were occurring. Driving his ancient black Chevrolet coupe early one afternoon on November 1, 1950, Beltrante learned from his police monitor that there had been a shooting close by the White House, which was then undergoing remodeling. In fact, the gunshots had rung out in front of Blair House, where, as everyone then knew, President Harry Truman was temporarily staying.

After racing to the scene, Beltrante found the body of Secret Service agent Leslie Coffelt lying on the sidewalk. He had been shot by a hail of bullets flying from a 9mm Luger wielded by a Puerto Rican nationalist who wanted independence for his homeland. Beltrante tried to revive the agent—without success. "He was already dead," he recalls grimly. The brutal homicide was a shock, but so was the scene that unfolded: the powerful and the protected suddenly so vulnerable. "Harry Truman stuck his head out of the damn upstairs window to see what was going on, and one of the Secret Service men who'd just come out of the building started yelling, 'Back in, Mr. President!! Back in!'"

Ruefully, the old policeman shakes his head. He loved Harry Truman—"Truman was my favorite president of all, a down-to-earth guy," Beltrante likes to say. But

"Mr. President, care to go for a ride in a police cruiser?"

"No, you guys just keep on going," Truman replied. "I'm out for my early morning constitutional."

Truman was also, he concedes, a trial. Almost six decades ago, Beltrante was driving around on a summer night in his patrol car along the broad expanse of Washington's Constitution Avenue when, he recalls, "I looked over to the right, and who was walking down the street? President Harry Truman."

Truman was completely alone. There was no security. It was 3 a.m.

"Mr. President, care to go for a ride in a police cruiser?" asked Beltrante.

"No, you guys just keep on going," Truman replied. "I'm out for my early-morning constitutional." And off he went to continue his stroll. "He was notorious for slipping out of the White House and going out for a walk; he would just sneak out," says Beltrante. "Needless to say, I was very concerned."

He learned the habits and quirks of presidents pretty well. When Dwight D. Eisenhower went to church or gave a speech at a hotel, Beltrante was either seated right behind him in plainclothes or standing close by, a tiny button on his lapel that functioned as a microphone. When John F. Kennedy surprised him by winning the national election, Beltrante popped up by his side at one of the inaugural balls—and consistently thereafter, whenever he was making a public appearance in Washington.

Always when on these details, he'd walk through a grim mental calculus. "I'd say to myself, 'Now, how could someone shoot him?' I'd look around and have different scenarios in my mind as to how that could be done," he says. Certain presidents were much harder to keep safe than others. "Kennedy was especially difficult," says Beltrante. "He would just dash into the crowd and wouldn't give us an opportunity to stick with him! He was what I would call reckless." The bottom line was this: "In each instance,

I could always find a way. I just felt it was not possible to give 100 percent security to a president of the United States."

When Beltrante retired in July 1963, his new career as a private investigator was almost as varied: corrupt entrepreneurs, errant husbands, runaway teenagers. He had what was needed: patience, persistence and, most of all, discretion. After Watergate, he had the fame, too. So there was politics. Always politics.

After plugged-in politicians learned of Beltrante's debugging efforts on behalf of McGovern, the detective was much in demand. Both the flamboyant Democratic Congresswoman Bella Abzug of New York and her colleague Elizabeth Holtzman (another New York Democrat) requested his services, he says. Only Abzug's congressional phones proved interesting to the detective. "A strange thing happened: We could hear conversations on her phones, the very people who were tapping her phones," says Beltrante. In a divided town, he was popular with Republicans, too. Four years after Watergate, he was hired by Gerald Ford's election committee to screen applicants for important strategy posts.

One year ago, at age 80, Beltrante sold his beloved business, by then an eponymous firm. He was, he says, burned out. In retirement, he often asks himself why he happened to become the Zelig of Washington, around whenever anything important occurred. "It is interesting to reflect on," he says slowly. "I have no idea why, though. Just chance, I think."

Well, perhaps not entirely chance. For years, he's been examining the murky circumstances surrounding the assassination of John F. Kennedy, the man Beltrante first met when just a young cop on the beat. "I'll be working on that one till I die," he promises. ❧

Welcome Home

by CHRIS SMITH

illustrations by SCOTT JOHNSON

THE ONLY THING THAT WAS CALM THAT MORNING WAS THE GULF OF Mexico waters. And thank goodness for that: Oscar C. de Tuya had barely set foot in a boat during his 36 years of life, and now here he was steering a secondhand, sputtering 33-foot Chris-Craft across the 140 miles from Marathon Key to Cuba. Yet, while the seas were luckily serene, everything else in de Tuya's world was in utter turmoil.

Cuba, his homeland, was being roiled by the violent aftermath of Fidel Castro's revolution. Thousands of political opponents had been killed as Castro swung from democratic guerrilla leader to Communist dictator. Still more Cubans had been imprisoned,

often on the flimsiest of charges. Among them had been Oscar de Tuya, seized one afternoon in 1960 for no apparent reason and tossed into a moldering, overcrowded, 18th-century Spanish fort called La Cabana, which had been converted into a brutal, makeshift prison for Castro's enemies, real and imagined. "After a few months, with no charges and no explanation, I figured the only way I was getting out would be in a wooden box," he says. But after nearly a year behind bars, de Tuya was sprung as suddenly and inexplicably as he'd been jailed. That night, he hid out at a friend's house, lest the authorities change their minds and come looking for him at home; three days later, de Tuya was on a flight from Havana to Miami.

Now, five years later, he was on his way back for the first time, his heart thrumming with fear and hope. His father, Oscar de Tuya, Sr., had spent five years in La Cabana. He'd been convicted in a sham trial of being a spy for the United States — with the strongest "evidence" being a photograph of the de Tuyas, father and son, grinning in a Havana restaurant where they'd had a chance encounter with the American ambassador. Oscar, Sr., 69 years old, was sentenced to 12 years in prison. However, a series of random kindnesses and favors had led to his early release. Castro, in one of his bursts of anger and calculation, had declared that anyone who wanted to flee the country was free to go. For the moment, anyway.

When word reached Oscar, Jr., in Miami, he wasted no time planning to rescue his father, mother and grandmother. What he didn't have was money: The de Tuyas lost their prosperous shipping business when Castro took over, and Oscar, Jr., was pumping gas for a dollar an hour in a Gulf station in Miami, feeding his wife and daughter on a maximum of $90 a week. He saw an ad for a used boat in a local paper, and begged and pleaded with his exile friends, borrowing $3,000 to buy the *French Twist* from a hair-dresser in Boca Raton. Just after dark on an October night, he set off, with a mechanic friend from the Gulf station, into the Gulf of Mexico, with navigational charts he couldn't really read and a rudimentary understanding of the compass beside the boat's steering wheel. "Neither the mechanic nor I had ever been on a boat," de Tuya says. "We thought we'd end up in Jamaica or who knows where."

Twelve hours later, the sun was rising, and he could make out some land on the horizon. Was that a stand of palm trees? They looked very much like the palm trees he'd passed on the way to the beach as a boy. But was that wishful thinking? His mind raced: Even if they'd found the right island, would he be able to find his family? What condition would his father be in after five rough years in a Communist prison? Would Castro really allow them all to leave? Or would they look up Oscar, Jr.'s prison record and lock him up again?

Moments later, one of his questions was answered. He was definitely back in Cuba: Soldiers were boarding his boat, rifles slung over their shoulders. Welcome home.

....

Oscar de Tuya will tell you, repeatedly, that he's an ordinary man. He'll tell you, with equal sincerity, that the most exciting moment of his life was pursuing a lawsuit all the way to the U.S. Supreme Court and winning, in a 1985 case that lifted onerous union burdens from small companies in the freight-forwarding industry.

What he will never say is that he's a genuine hero, even though he'd be entirely justified. Oscar de Tuya is too humble for that kind of boasting. And humility is one of the primary qualities underlying his brave actions back in 1965; together with fierce loyalty to his family and an unyielding optimism, humility also enabled de Tuya to build a successful second life out of a nightmare that left many of his fellow exiles consumed by bitterness. Instead, at 79, he's white-haired, stoop-shouldered and slight, with merry brown eyes that say Oscar de Tuya cherishes the chance the United States gave him.

It also helps that de Tuya possesses a finely tuned, ironic sense of humor. "Castro is from my school. He graduated two years before me, class of '45," de Tuya says. "I used to know the guy, from sports, basketball and baseball. He was very smart, a good student." Their mutual alma mater, a Jesuit secondary school called El Colegio de Belén, was one of the finest in Cuba, so revered that its graduates were allowed to skip the entrance exams for American colleges. "The priest who prepares the yearbook wrote about Fidel, 'We have no doubt that he will write brilliant pages in the history of Cuba,'" de Tuya says with a sharp laugh. "I saw the priest years later in Miami. He said, 'Well, my son, we all make mistakes!' He sure did. It doesn't make any sense that a guy from one of the best Jesuit schools could become such a crazy radical."

De Tuya learned long ago not to expect life to make sense, and to make the most of random fortune, good or bad. After graduating from high school, he was planning to study journalism at Columbia University in New York, until the day he went to a drive-in with his girlfriend. "I was having a chocolate shake and the lottery ticket man came up," de Tuya says. "He said, 'Listen, I have a ticket with the number of the license of your car: 33584.' I'll never forget that number. I'd never bought a ticket before, but I bought this one and put it in the glove compartment and forgot about it." Ten days later, de Tuya won $100,000. "That was a lot of money in 1948 in a country like Cuba! I said the hell with Columbia! My father was mad; we had quite a struggle."

Oscar, Sr., had left school as a teenager, going to work to support his mother and siblings after his own father died suddenly. He eventually built Tuya Cuban Express from scratch into the country's largest international freight-forwarding firm. Oscar, Sr., was apolitical, though his son says he hated dictatorship of any kind, and so welcomed Castro's toppling of the corrupt regime of General Fulgencio Batista. "We thought Fidel was going to be a savior," de Tuya says. "But two months after he took over, whoever had a brain was very doubtful, when you see he starts lining people up against the wall and shooting them for no reason."

And it wasn't long before the elder de Tuya's business dealings with U.S. companies made him a target of the new dictator.

....

Castro's secret police went first to the de Tuya house. But father and son were at the office, working late. The phone rang. "My father comes and says, 'Your mother called. She says men from the G2 were at the house asking for me. And now they're coming to the office.'"

The terror washes across Oscar de Tuya's face, all these years later. "I pushed my father down the stairs," he says. "As we were running out of the building, two cars arrived. 'Oscar de Tuya?' 'Yeah.' 'Please come with us.'" The son was allowed to walk away that night; one week later, however, while he was consulting with a lawyer about how to free his father, the G2 stormed in and handcuffed Oscar, Jr.—along with the lawyer, who had been a comrade of Castro's but broke with him after the revolution turned vindictive. De Tuya and the lawyer were taken to the quarters of an army chief and harangued at length; the lawyer crumbled. "He got on the floor, on his knees—'No!

No! It's a mistake! Nothing happened!' I thought the guy was going to cry," de Tuya says, the disgust in his voice fresh. "I said, 'I can't believe this! This might be a tough situation. They might shoot us. But you have to die like a man!'"

That same pride and dignity sustained both de Tuyas in prison. "I slept for two weeks on the floor. It's bad, but it doesn't kill you," de Tuya says. "They put me on the same cellblock where my father was. When they opened the prison yard in the morning, my father would go out and scream at the soldiers: 'You son-of-a-bitch Communists! Get out of here!' The other prisoners would say, 'Oscar, you're going to get shot!' He'd say, 'I don't give a damn!'" De Tuya laughs. "My father was quite a character."

So when the slim chance came to rescue him, as well as de Tuya's mother and grandmother, there was no hesitation. De Tuya's brother, Jorge, younger by 14 years, had escaped to Miami in 1960; he insisted on accompanying Oscar on the mission, and they fought all night before Oscar left Marathon Key. "I told him, 'No, Jorge. I'm the older one in the family, it's my responsibility to bring the father. If they get me when I get there because they look at the records and see I was in prison, well, bad luck. But it's my responsibility.'" There was also the small matter of the American embargo, which didn't permit such private journeys to the Communist enemy nation. "I broke the law going to Cuba, but what can you do?" de Tuya says. "You have your father, your mother — the hell with the law. You go and pick them up."

A couple of miles away from Camarioca, a very small town with an inlet, de Tuya was met by the Cuban coast guard and directed to follow them into the port. After arriving at Camarioca, de Tuya was detained for three weeks, and got a glimpse of what had become of his homeland. He was held, along with other would-be rescuers, in the former mansion of one of Cuba's richest men; it had been converted into a revolutionary school for laborers, with cooking fires burning in bathroom sinks. As the days stretched on, de Tuya didn't lose hope, but he began to wonder if the government's whims had changed again and he'd never see his family.

Then one morning, down at the pier where de Tuya had tied his battered boat, a bus pulled up. Off it stepped his grandmother, his mother and a man he recognized, but barely. "He was wearing my brother's old clothes," de Tuya says quietly. "My father came out of prison in very bad shape. He'd lost 40 or 50 pounds. He came and hugged me. That was quite a meeting."

Not that the solemnity lasted long. "My father started yelling about the Communists!" de Tuya says, chuckling. "I told him, 'Wait 10 minutes, until we're on the boat and out of here!'" As the boat chugged out into the Gulf, he looked back. "I don't remember my last image of Cuba," he says. "What I remember are my tears. I said, 'This is going to be the last time that I'm going to see my country.' Seeing the port of Cuba, the mountains, it was sad. I cried. I cried."

On the trip back to Florida, de Tuya saved a fellow traveler, a Cuban adrift in a boat whose engine had failed. Still, he shrugs off the whole extraordinary adventure as something any decent person would do. "I'm an ordinary man. I have some stories, things that haven't happened to everybody, but it doesn't make me a hero. I'm just a Cuban who came here and worked very hard." With his brother, de Tuya created an American version of the family's shipping business, a company that far outgrew the Cuban original. His only regret is that their father didn't live long enough to see his boys' triumph: Oscar de Tuya died 11 months after arriving in America. Thanks to his first-born son, though, he died a free man. ∾

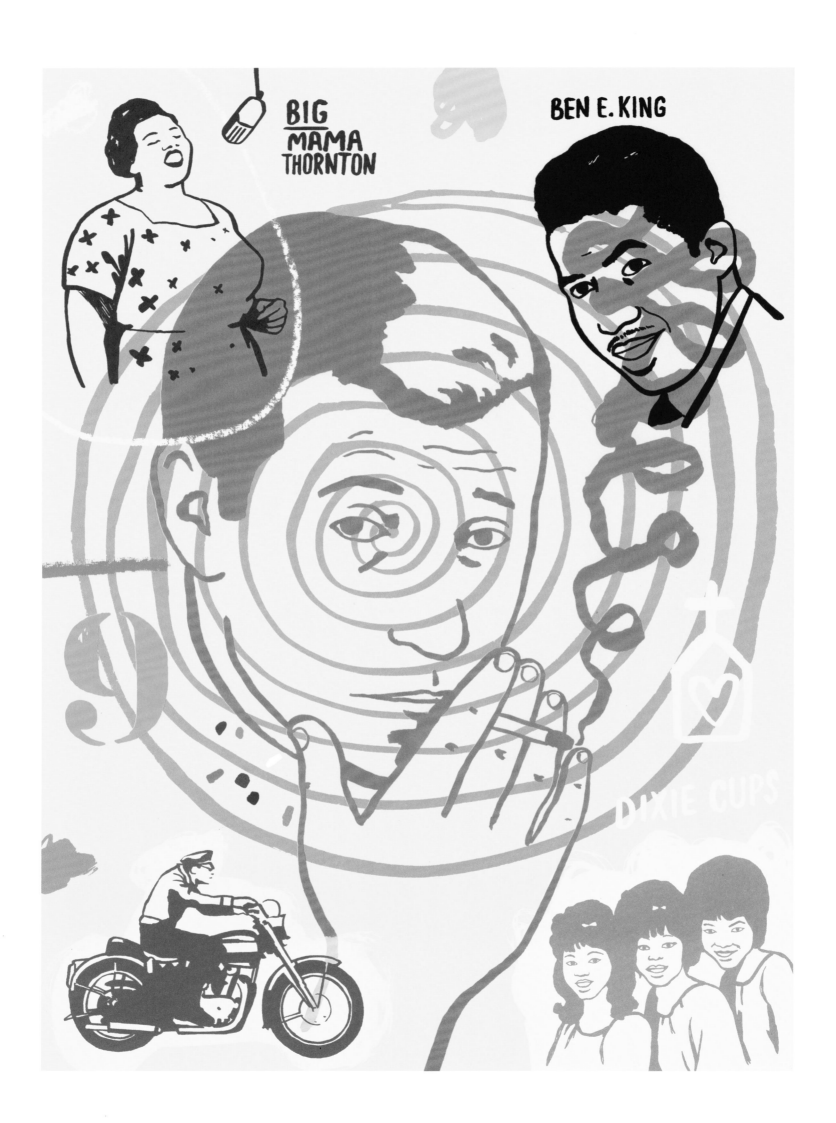

IS THAT ALL THERE IS?

by DAVID RITZ

illustrations by BRIAN CAIRNS

NINETEEN SIXTY-NINE WAS A HELL OF A YEAR FOR POPULAR MUSIC: The 5th Dimension ushering in the "Age of Aquarius," the Stones celebrating "Honky Tonk Women," the Beatles urging us to "Get Back" and "Come Together." The truth is that we were both coming and going. Peter, Paul and Mary were "Leaving on a Jet Plane," while Diana Ross and the Supremes promised "Someday We'll Be Together." It was, to say the least, a confusing time. The hippie era had far from flagged, and, yet, as Elvis reminded us with his "Suspicious Minds," a hit that same year, unrest was everywhere.

Cultural collisions were hardly novelties for lyricist Jerry Leiber and his partner Mike Stoller, who gained fame as white guys writing black songs. In that role, they had been innovators since the early 1950s. They had written for everyone from Ray Charles to the Coasters. Their initial rhythm-and-blues success, "Hound Dog," sung originally by Big Mama Thornton only to be reinterpreted by Elvis, was one of the great pillars upon which rock and roll was built. In the early 1960s, they scored big with love anthems like "Stand by Me" and street anthems like "On Broadway."

"By the end of the decade, though," says Leiber, "our minds and hearts had moved on to what seemed more serious matters."

Leiber settles back in a director's chair in his spacious home facing the Venice, California, promenade and a wide swathe of ocean beyond. He takes a deep breath before he starts to discuss what he terms "the turning point of all turning points in my ever-turning life." At 75, Leiber exudes the confident charm of a master storyteller. Like a jazzman, he tells his tales in short, punctuated riffs. His patois, a combination of hipster slang and poetic grace, is a language unto itself. You want to listen to him all night long. You also can't help but be drawn to his remarkably mismatched eyes: the right one is baby blue; the left, chestnut brown. He's quick to say that he's a nocturnal creature and, in fact, it's only when the sun sinks into the Pacific and the light of day turns dark that Leiber slips into his element.

"Before I get to that turning point in 1969," he says, "we need to rewind the tape to an earlier time. Remember that wave of songs that fought off the British Invasion in the early sixties? Most of those numbers were associated with the Girl Groups."

Leiber is referring to tunes like the Dixie Cups' "Chapel of Love" and the Shangri-Las' "Leader of the Pack," both released by Red Bird Records, the label owned by Leiber and Stoller. It was a time when the sensibilities of teenage girls were starting to claim the attention of the listening public.

"We appreciated the movement," Leiber reflects, "and we participated in its flowering, but our own aesthetic didn't have much to do with sock hops and bubble-gum romance. I was always drawn to the complexities and charms of the fully mature woman. In fact, our relationship with Peggy Lee—the heroine of the story I'm about to tell you—began with that very concept."

Peggy Lee's great diva-dom spanned six decades. She sang with Benny Goodman in the 1940s, cracked the hit parade with "Fever" in the 1950s and, in 1963, scored again with Leiber/Stoller's "I'm A Woman."

"I considered Peggy the best all-around female singer standing," says Leiber, "and the only one capable of rendering lyrics like …

If you come to me sickly, you know I'm gonna make you well.
If you come to me all hexed up, you know I'm gonna break the spell.
If you come to me hungry, you know I'll fill you full o' grits.
If it's lovin' you're lackin', I'll kiss ya and give ya the shiverin' fits,
'Cause I'm a woman — W. O. M. A. N.
I got a twenty-dollar gold piece says there ain't nothing I can't do,
I can make a dress out of a feed bag an' I can make a man out of you."

Leiber doesn't recite the words; he sings them — loudly and with conviction — and when he is through, he sings the song again, this time remembering the second verse that, he's quick to point out, places the composition outside the realm of the teenage mind:

I can run an' scrub till this old house is shinin' like a dime,
Feed the baby, grease the car an' powder my face at the same time,
Get all dressed up, go out an' swing till four a.m. and then
Lay down at five, jump up at six an' start all over again.

"I'm A Woman" was an anomaly: a grown-up song in the age of "Baby Love."

"Peggy was gratified to have a hit," says Leiber, "but Peggy was also Peggy. She followed a muse unknown to any of us. I thought she'd want more of our songs, but she disappeared from our world. Most of the decade passed without a word from her. The decade, of course, got crazier with time. Assassinations. War. Cultural chaos. I found myself reading writers I'd never read before. Thomas Mann was one. He wrote a story called 'Disillusionment' that knocked me for a loop. Its subject is the deep-down blues. The story motivated me to look deep into the existential hole that sits in the center

IS THAT ALL THERE IS
37F

of our souls. It also inspired me to write a series of loosely connected verses in which I envisioned a character, a disillusioned woman, speaking, not singing, words to this effect:

> *I remember when I was a little girl, our house caught on fire.*
> *I'll never forget the look on my father's face*
> *As he gathered me up in his arms*
> *And raced through the burning building out onto the pavement.*
> *I stood there shivering in my pajamas*
> *And watched the whole world go up in flames.*
> *When it was all over, I said to myself…*
> *Is that all there is to a fire,*
> *Is that all there is?"*

Three more verses came quickly to Leiber. The second was a childhood memory of a circus. Yet as exciting as the greatest show on earth might have been, it left our heroine with the same haunting question. The third verse concerned a love affair gone wrong, and the fourth verse, the most devastating of all, focused on what Leiber called the "final disappointment."

> *For I know just as well as I'm standing here talking to you,*
> *When that final moment comes and I'm breathing my last breath,*
> *I'll be saying to myself,*
> *Is that all there is?*

Stoller wrote the beautifully haunting music that underscores the spoken verses.

Enter Georgia Brown, an English singer-actress who was starring on Broadway in "Oliver!" She was returning to Great Britain to do a television show and needed special material. Leiber and Stoller played her their Kurt Weill-meets-Bertolt Brecht-styled song. The manager liked it, and so did Miss Brown, but she wanted more. She wanted a refrain—a chorus, a hook, something to anchor the song and, even more critically, something that would be sung, not merely spoken.

"We had a piece of another song that had been suspended in our imagination," says Leiber, "and we used it for the chorus. Georgia liked it, but we didn't. It just didn't fit. So I went home to write new lyrics, and Mike went home to write new music. Next morning, I went over to Mike's with lyrics that I knew were perfect. But the first thing Mike said was, 'I have music that I know is perfect. You'll have to make the words fit them.'

"'Or vice versa,' I countered. 'The lyrics are so right you can change the music to accommodate the words.'

"Mike said, 'Well, first let me play the music for you.' I said, 'No, first let *me* read you the lyrics.'

"We went back and forth for several minutes until I caved. When Mike played the music, I was astonished. 'Play it again,' I urged him. He did, and as he did I started singing the words I had written. They fit perfectly. In a relationship that has spanned six decades, this had never happened before and has never happened since."

After Georgia Brown performed the song on English television, Leiber had another idea: The perfect singer to record "Is That All There Is?" would be Marlene Dietrich. "After all," says Leiber, "the song sounds like it could have been written in the 1930s, Dietrich's heyday. And it contains all the angst that's the heart of her persona."

Through his friend Burt Bacharach, who was conducting for Dietrich, Leiber got an audience with the great diva. Bacharach played the song while Leiber sang it.

"Dietrich's reaction was beautiful," says Leiber. "In her regal manner, she walked over to me and said, 'Darling, this song is who I am, not what I do.'" Next stop, Barbra Streisand. But Streisand's manager didn't even bother playing her the song. He deemed it far too serious.

"Of course, the song always had Peggy Lee written all over it," says Leiber, "but given how Peggy had shown little interest in us, even after 'I'm A Woman,' Mike and I were reluctant."

Persistence trumped reluctance, though, and Leiber found himself face-to-face with the Grande Dame in her suite in the Waldorf Towers.

"Suite 37F," Leiber remembers. "There was a party going on. People everywhere. I caught sight of Peggy. I handed her the disc containing the demo, told her I thought that the song might be right for her, and that was that. A week later, she called back and said, 'I will kill you if you give this song to anyone but me. This is my song. This is the story of my life.'"

Of course, the song changed Lee's life, giving her sagging career a much-needed lift. Putting her performance on tape, however, was far from easy.

Leiber remembers: "In her late 40s, Peggy was experienced, sweet, salty, willing and resistant—all at once. Because she was a composer herself, she knew the ins and outs of a nuanced song, and because she loved this song so deeply, we prayed that the session would go smoothly. Randy Newman's arrangement was brilliant. The musicians arrived on time. Everything was in place. Peggy made a dramatic entrance, looking gorgeous and, in a discreet leather case, carried in a fifth of brandy. She placed the bottle nearby, but I never saw her take a drink.

"'I'm committed to doing three takes,' she said, 'and no more.'

"'That's cool, baby,' I said. 'Three takes should do it.'

"At take 10, we still didn't have it. Her interpretations, while always intelligent, hadn't found the precise ironic grace that defines the song. But being a trouper, Peggy kept going, realizing that a masterpiece was within reach. At take 15, I suspect she took a belt because her readings were improving. Take 30 was good, but take 36 was pure magic. I looked at Mike and Mike looked at me, and it was all we could do not to jump up and down with joy. This was one of the greatest performances either one of us had ever heard, in or out of a recording studio. Peggy had done it. We had done it. The enormous potential in this strange little song had been realized.

"'Let's hear it back,' I told the engineer.

"We waited. Silence. We waited a little longer. More silence.

"'What's wrong?' asked Peggy. 'I'm dying to hear that last take.'

"Then came the words from the engineer that cut through me like a knife. 'I didn't hit the record button.'

"'*What do you mean, you didn't hit the record button?*' I screamed at the top of my lungs.

"'*You had to have hit the record button. This was the greatest take in the history of takes! Stop joking! Let's hear it! Play the goddamn thing!*'

"But there was nothing to play. Nothing to do. Nothing had been recorded. Killing this kid would have been too kind. Yet, Peggy, bless her heart, was stoic. 'Guess I'll just have to sing it again,' she said bravely. And she did. Take 37 was nothing short of marvelous. That's the take the world knows today. She is melancholy, she is sultry, she is fatalistic, she is in tune and she delivers the song with a wondrous sense of mystery. It is good — it is, in fact, very, very good — but is not, nor will it ever be, take 36."

Capitol Records was not impressed.

"Peggy was viewed as passé," says Leiber. "Fact is, Capitol Records was about to drop her from the label. We figured, *what the hell, we'd written a great song, she'd sung it beautifully, but it was a lost cause.* Maybe someone would slip the thing in the time capsule and it'd be rediscovered by a race of white aborigines in year 3002. Capitol refused to release it."

Fate intervened. Capitol Records wanted to place two of its young artists on Joey Bishop's TV talk show. Joey agreed, but only if he could also host Peggy. Peggy agreed, but only if Capitol released "Is That All There Is?" Capitol relented, pressing only 1,500 copies. Peggy appeared on the show and sang the song, if not as well as take 36, good enough to cause a tidal wave of calls. The record sold out within hours; more copies were pressed; then more, and even more, until the song soared to the top tier of the *Billboard* chart, where it remained for two months. Not only was "Is That All There Is?" an international hit in the last quarter of 1969, it transcended the mere temporal and entered the sacred realm of the eternal, becoming a standard that is sure to be played forever and a day.

....

It's growing late in Venice. Leiber gets up from the director's chair and surveys the scene outside his home. Other than an isolated couple walking along the water's edge, the beach is deserted. The ocean reflects the white light of the moon and a sky crowded with stars.

"Mike and I were asked to perform the song the other night at a benefit concert," he says. "I hadn't sung it in years. But when I did, I felt its power all over again. For all the millions of times that I've heard it, the song felt as new and fresh as the day Mike and I wrote it. And perhaps most amazing was the revelation that, in reciting the verses and singing the chorus, I knew that, while it's no doubt the story of Peggy Lee's life, it's the story of mine as well." ❧

Take My Hand

by SUSAN CHOI

illustrations by LAURA CARLIN

THE NAACP LEADERS AT HEADQUARTERS IN NEW YORK CITY HAD gotten word from state leaders in Arkansas that some moral support might be needed in Hoxie. It was 1955, and Hoxie meant to integrate its schools, supposedly in response to Brown v. Board of Education but really in response to their own lack of funds. It was expensive to keep up separate schools for black and white children. Mildred Bond Roxborough was then a two-year veteran of the NAACP, but it was not her experience that qualified her for Hoxie, in the opinion of Thurgood Marshall. Marshall, then the organization's special counsel, said of Bond Roxborough, "Well, she's young. Send her!"

In Hoxie, she was hosted by one of the handful of black families in town whose children were about to make their foray into the previously whites-only elementary school. The house was exceedingly modest, with an outhouse at the far end of the backyard. The property abutted that of a white family, whose outhouse was also at the far end of their backyard. And so the two privies, like the yards, were back-to-back; and in similar mirror fashion, the white family was also playing host to out-of-town visitors drawn by the imminent attempt at integration, in their case representatives of an organization whose name, White America, summed up their agenda.

But Bond Roxborough was no more scared of using the outhouse than of anything else that might be involved in maintaining the morale of the parents and, most important, their children. "They were grade-school children," she points out. "Not like at Central High." And so the first day, and for most of a month afterward, she marched her young charges to school, through the sweltering heat and, of course, the protesters. To keep the huddle of small people moving she might say, "It's hot! Let's get out of this heat!" Or, more seriously, "It's important that you go to school. You must not be afraid."

There couldn't have been anyone better to lead by example. As a child herself, only eight years old, Bond Roxborough had been home alone one night in Brownsville, Tennessee, waiting for her mother to return from a meeting, when her father arrived instead, deposited in the living room by the sheriff and his deputy. "Your pa's been injured," one of them commented. "You'd better take care of him." Ollie Bond, a native of Brownsville, graduate of Lane College, veteran of the First World War, and leading light of Brownsville's black community—he and his wife, Mattye, had organized the town's chapter of the NAACP—had in fact been bludgeoned with brass knuckles. It was only the most recent in a series of reprisals that had been steadily escalating for the year and a half since Ollie and Mattye had begun organizing Brownsville's blacks to demand what they were entitled to by law, but denied by local government throughout Haywood County: the right to vote. Bond Roxborough followed Ollie's instructions for bandaging his cracked head until Mattye came home.

Not long after, while Mattye was away on an emergency visit to a relative in Kansas City, word came from the local coroner, a white man who was also a relative, that Ollie was going to be murdered. The town was full of tangled kinships between blacks and whites, half-brothers and half-sisters, some of whom could scarcely be distinguished racially. "It's something everybody knew. You didn't pay attention to it. It was a fact of life," Bond Roxborough says. Just as it was a fact of life that the coroner—whose white father was also her paternal great-grandfather—could warn the family that Ollie was going to be killed but could do nothing himself to prevent this. He was not even expected to try.

In one concession to the crisis, Mildred was sent to a relative's, but Ollie refused to hide. It was Christmas Eve. Finally, Ollie's mother—the coroner's half-sister—prevailed on Ollie to come to her home outside town. That night, unaware that the house was abandoned, Ollie's enemies burned it to the ground. The next morning, Christmas, only the three chimneys of Bond Roxborough's childhood home still stood. Everyone assumed Ollie had perished inside, until the ashes were sifted. It turned out Ollie had made his way from his mother's house to Mattye, in Kansas City. Soon Bond Roxborough followed.

So, by 1955, she already knew about fear, not to mention starting school somewhere new under bad circumstances. But say "fear"— or "courage"—and she'll pshaw the individual emotion or virtue away. "It's funny how you can live under crisis," she concludes cheerfully. As if regretting employing the word *crisis* in her own minor tale, she also says, "This was not an unusual story. You understand that. But," she laughs, "it becomes personal, of course, when it's you!"

One stands like the spindle around which rotates a vast, flat disk of soil. A single tree is as starkly expressive as the cornfield's scarecrow.

You might run a long distance and still be very easily found in the sights of a gun.

Mildred Bond Roxborough is quick to laugh — and slow, perhaps even constitution-ally averse, to dwelling upon her personal emotions or accomplishments. She would much rather detail the situations that were and the work that was done and the chal-lenges that remain and the organizational structures through which we might face them. But it doesn't make sense to say she is modest — modesty is too dainty a virtue. Perhaps one can say she seems a stranger to self-centered modes of thought. She seems never to have wondered, *What do I want? What am I like? What are my needs?* Instead she has gravitated, from the very beginning, with eager energy and great capacity, toward the doings and needs of her fellows.

Back in Brownsville, her early enthusiasm for the NAACP magazine *The Crisis* — she had learned to read well before kindergarten, seated on her mother's lap while Mattye read aloud to her two older sisters — had turned into an enthusiasm for disseminating *The Crisis* to others. The magazine contained news of black people all over the country, as well as verses by such writers as Paul Laurence Dunbar and Langston Hughes. Per-haps most interesting of all, it retailed for a nickel. Why could Bond Roxborough not sell it and enlighten her fellows? At age nine, she did still require some small assistance from her mother in drafting a letter to Roy Wilkins, who was the magazine's editor and later the NAACP president. But her qualifications to become a subscription agent for the magazine, which was the favor her letter requested, were apparently plain from a distance. Mr. Wilkins kindly granted permission, and even offered commission.

....

To this same Roy Wilkins, it must have seemed that Bond Roxborough was destined to work for the NAACP. After all, it was Wilkins who some two decades later agreed with Thurgood Marshall that she should go down to Hoxie. To a casual observer, Bond Roxborough's more than half-century of service to the NAACP since

1953 (she is still a daily presence in the New York office since her alleged retirement in 1996) might suggest the same basic idea. But this wasn't her thinking at all. "Work for the NAACP?" she says. "It never occurred to me—I never thought about it!"

Perhaps because she had been the sort of nine-year-old prone to exhorting her neighbors that they should read *The Crisis* for its "news of what's happening to us all over the country!", by her 20s, Bond Roxborough had lifted her sights from the national stage to the global, from her people to all people. In the course of completing a bachelor's degree at New York University and a master's at Columbia, she had lived in France and Mexico, working in clinics and teaching under the auspices of the American Friends Service Committee. AFSC had so impressed her that she'd decided to make her career with that organization, "serving people, and bringing people together" all over the world. To better do so, she was headed to pick up a doctorate in social psychology at Columbia—but then the NAACP started calling her.

While Bond Roxborough had been attending college, one of her older sisters had started working for the NAACP. Of course, their parents, Ollie and Mattye, had long been known to the organization. Was it possible someone remembered Bond Roxborough's zeal selling *The Crisis* subscriptions? Now the association's director of branches and field administration wanted her to manage a membership and fundraising campaign in Baltimore. When she balked—after all, Columbia awaited—the director assured her it was only a short-term commitment. She'd be finished in time to start school in the fall. Soon Bond Roxborough's parents were cajoling her, too. "He needed a body," she laughs, waving off the suggestion that what the director needed was what he saw in her: a veritable genius of energy, commitment and organization.

She never made it back to Columbia. After Baltimore came the Brown decision in 1954, and soon Bond Roxborough was traveling to Hoxie. "It was infectious, you see."

The NAACP leaders at headquarters in New York City had gotten word from state leaders in Mississippi that urgent assistance was required in the Delta. Local blacks there, many of them farmers, were attempting to vote. "It was the same old story," Bond Roxborough remembers. "Economic reprisals. Denied credit for the winter, so you can't get your groceries." And worse. She set out "to get the farmers' experiences. Have them recount for us what was happening to them, how they were managing to survive. In other words, to get their testimony." Thus armed, the association would secure outside financial assistance for the farmers: The first order of business was that no one starve. Bond Roxborough's companion was an NAACP field officer named Medgar Evers.

In the Delta, that desolate floodplain of the wandering Mississippi, there is nowhere to hide. One stands like the spindle around which rotates a vast, flat disk of soil. A single tree is as starkly expressive as the cornfield's scarecrow. You might run a long distance and still be very easily found in the sights of a gun. Bond Roxborough and Evers worked by night. Partly they did this because farmers are busy by day, but they had other reasons. Together they would drive the country roads, through nights black as the bowels of a cave. In towns like Yazoo City, they found small groups awaiting them at a gathering point, which was usually a church. Each interview subject would sign his or her statement, or, as often would happen if the person had not learned to write, ask Bond Roxborough for help. Then she would place her hand over that person's, and guide it along.

Afterward was the long, dark drive back to Mound Bayou, where the black motel was—a single room with the bath down the hall, and in the room a single bed and a lumpy settee. Bond Roxborough and Evers tossed a coin to see who got the bed. Even getting stuck with the settee was more restful than accepting hospitality from people in the Delta, because this only further endangered their lives. As Bond Roxborough knew, she and Medgar were the primary targets. Not long after their travels together, Medgar Evers was killed by an assassin's bullet.

Yet she was rarely afraid in the moment. "In doing it, in going across those fields at night…when I first went in there, my stomach was queasy. And then you start doing it, and you don't have time to think." She pauses, thinking of it now. "You might get frightened after the fact," she concedes, continuing to use the second person, to deflect emphasis from herself and her irrelevant feelings. "Afterward you might think, *Wasn't I a fool! How could I have done that?*"

But she spends little time looking back. A lucky interviewer might pass a most amazing few hours discussing with Bond Roxborough not just the organization to which she's devoted decades of her life, but all the nations she's seen as the wife of a member of the foreign service; all the novels, plays, musicals and chamber music recitals she has adored; all the dear friends ("non-NAACP!") who enliven her days; all the projects she has planned for her real retirement ("all good things must come to an end")—only to blunder by asking if there's one thing of which she's most proud. This is just the kind of self-inflating mode of thought that seems most to annoy her. "It's hard to think about being proud of yourself," she says, not with humility but with a touch of admonishment.

"Glad?" the interviewer amends, timidly. She thinks a moment.

"I'm, ah, *pleased*. I feel a certain amount of…gratification, that I have been able to be in a place, at times, where I was needed."

But Mildred Bond Roxborough, who has been known to dress in chic, tailored separates in coordinating shades of ravishing fuchsia, can't stay stern for too long. "I think it's made me a better person," she admits of her astonishing career. Then she bursts into gales of laughter. "Well, I hope that it has!" ❧

The Heart of Hollywood

by SHEILA WELLER

illustrations by JOSIE JAMMET

W HEN ARMY ARCHERD, THE VENERABLE PETRARCH OF HOLLYWOOD, and his wife Selma, get to the Beverly Hills Hotel parking-court curb right after dinner, their car is already there: doors open, motor humming — a uniformed attendant has seen them striding out the portico and has fetched the car, unasked. "We wouldn't dream of requesting that kind of treatment," says Selma, surrounded by other Polo Lounge diners, all dutifully proffering their validated tickets. "But people do things like this because Army is so respected. I would say he is the best-liked person in this city. For his decency. For his hard work."

And, one might add, for his heart. Army Archerd loves Hollywood, and he has championed its glamour, generosity and industriousness for five-and-a-half decades. Since 1953, his column, "Just for *Variety*," has been what members of the L.A. entertainment community first turn to as their coffee brews and the bougainvillea splashes dew on their kitchen windowpanes. There, on the green-logoed shiny sheet, in the spiffy patois he helped coin (a.m. is "ayem"; sensational is "sensaysh"; scheduled is "skedded") are items, separated by three dots, that range from production deals to juicy couplings. Whether business or romantic, it's news that's always true (in 55 years, he's not had to issue a single retraction) and never cruel. Viewed in retrospect, the columns report history. They began in the Korean War era, when stars actually served in the military: "April 28, 1953. Good morning. Vic Damone … heads for Texas this weekend to get his army discharge." They've witnessed changes in sensitive parts of the globe: "January 29, 1959. Good morning. It may grieve Desi Arnaz to hear it, but his *I Love Lucy* isn't very popular in Cuba, neither with the Batista nor Castro regimes." They've mourned senseless tragedies: "June 6, 1968: It's not a good morning in Hollywood…. The shock and sorrow of Hollywood" over Bobby Kennedy's assassination at the Ambassador Hotel "perhaps tops" that of "any community in the nation." All classic Archerd: a lover's steadfast journal of the town he moved to from the Bronx as a teenager in 1939, showing how much a strand—albeit a sparkly, sequined strand—of the fabric of America Hollywood really is.

But Army's only half of why people in Hollywood love Army. The other half is Selma Fenning Archerd: acerbic, witty, fun-loving former actress (she was Nurse Amy on *Melrose Place* and was in *Die Hard* and *Lethal Weapons I* and *III*) with Barbara Walters looks and theatrical diction. She is his confidante, best friend and fellow advocate. "Together, Army and Selma are the best cheerleaders anyone could possibly hope for, and Army's support, through his column, has been invaluable to all of us who work in the movie industry," say married couple Sherry Lansing and Billy Friedkin, powerhouses in the '70s through '90s. (Lansing was the first female studio head; Friedkin directed *The Exorcist* and *The French Connection*.) The Archerds are also, Lansing and Friedkin add, "good friends and great company." And not just to others, but to each other. "We've had a fabulous marriage for 38 years! We've had the most magnificent ride!" Selma enthuses. "The places we've gone! The parties we've given! The people we know!" She pauses. "Army and I really care about each other—we are soulmates." "Yes, we are," Army agrees, in soft, serious counterpoint to her vivid exclamations. A lifelong questioner of others, he chooses his own words warily when a reporter questions him. But Selma limns their bond: "When I call him at the office, he always says, 'Oh, I'm so glad it's you.'"

"We met at a UCLA fraternity party when we were very young," Army says. Selma: "I was a teenager! In bobby sox!" He was an amused, nonchalant Errol Flynn look-alike ("No, Tyrone Power," Selma corrects); she, the pretty ("No, *stunning*," Army insists) blonde daughter of a fur merchant: both transplants, he from New York and she from New Jersey. After a brief romance, they were separated by parents (hers felt she was much too young to be dating anyone seriously) and World War II (he served as a lieutenant). Each married someone else. Each had two children (Selma's are Richard and James; Army's are Amanda and Evan). Each divorced. When they met again in their early prime, they were like a wine that was finally correctly aged. The day after our Polo Lounge dinner, Selma, at home, points to their 1969 wedding picture. She has the chic, teased hair, the Jackie Kennedy dress; he is dapper, slyly adoring. "People called us a golden couple," she says.

Sadly, I am meeting with Army and Selma just days after a member of their circle, Cyd Charisse, has died. Army was, of course, the first columnist to learn, and write, of her death. Like Army and Selma—and like their friends Kirk and Anne Douglas, and the late Gregory Peck and his wife Veronique—Cyd Charisse and Tony Martin embodied a marital longevity virtually unknown in today's Hollywood. The Archerds recall the Martins' 50th anniversary party, and they muse that every single night for years "Cyd and Tony took a walk—their constitutional—to Hamlet Gardens for dinner," Selma says.

The reference is a pebble that goes down a long, sentimental chute. I grew up in this intimate, small-town, workaday old Hollywood where people took their meals at the various Hamburger Hamlet restaurants (a kind of L.A. version of Manhattan's Schrafft's).

My uncle owned the luminous nightclub Ciro's—Army sat at a ringside table every Tuesday and Friday night, scouting celebrity romances. My mother was a movie magazine editor; Army moonlighted, writing columns for her. And as I sit in the breakfast nook of the Archerds' Wilshire Corridor high-rise apartment—all shiny L.A.-luxe: Louis Quatorze chairs, dark wood floors, crystal chandeliers; Army's office lined with leatherbound *Daily Variety*s, plaques and awards, and a huge collage of matchbooks from legendary watering holes (the Stork Club, Mocambo, the Copa, Sardi's, Ciro's, the Luau, the Sands...)—eating cottage cheese and cantaloupe with Selma, it all feels so familiar.

Today, Hollywood is full of hip deal-makers speaking *Entourage*-ese; of stars in sweat pants, juggling lattes, cell phones and babies. "Movie stars aren't special anymore," Army complains. "They don't look like you want to spend money to see them." "In the old days, you certainly never saw photos of movie stars pregnant in bikinis! Back then, fans didn't even know stars *had* children," Selma says. But this vanished Hollywood—this elegant, shrewd, gutsy place—that was my childhood home. It is what Army has documented in his column, and it is what his and Selma's marriage celebrates.

Army's proudest scoop, and most important story, came in 1985: the revelation that Rock Hudson had AIDS. Nobody famous and beloved had ever been linked to the stigmatized, whispered-about disease. But Army had, months earlier, been shown Hudson's medical records by a source he will not name. "Still," Selma says, "Army sat on the story, even while Rock was kissing Doris Day on TV tribute shows." ("It's not worth ruining a life for a column," says Army, who has also seen famously "happily married" male movie VIPs in restaurants with women not their wives and, out of kindness to those wives, kept tomb-silent.) Only when Army knew Hudson was dying did he print the item. It garnered worldwide headlines and put a human face on the disease, greatly helping to destigmatize it and educate the public. Army has broken happy personal scoops, as well: His column informed a disbelieving Hollywood, in March 1992, that ultra-confirmed bachelor Warren Beatty had married Annette Bening. ("It was like hearing that the sound barrier had been broken," Army quips, "and Warren, who is *very* private, loves to remind me that I was the one who did that.") And industry job-quakes:

Back in 1968, he announced that minor actor Bob Evans was going to be made head of production at Paramount. "Everyone said I was out of my mind," he recalls. But Army's information was right, and Evans became a glamorous, golden-gutted powerhouse in 1970s-1980s Hollywood.

But despite such high-minded coups, Army started out in the 1940s gathering gamier dish, as a twentysomething who'd had three years on the L.A. Associated Press desk. He was hired as the legman for the L.A. *Herald-Express*'s gossip columnist Harrison Carroll. Carroll was underdog to gossip divas Louella Parsons and Hedda Hopper, so Army had to work harder: The maître d' at my uncle's Ciro's would call Army whenever a fight had broken out—and he'd dash down. And Army was there on Oscar night 1950, when an unknown Sammy Davis, Jr., became a star in front of everyone's delighted eyes. Davis had been the most junior member of the song-and-dance troupe the Will Mastin Trio, and they'd opened for Ciro's headliner Janis Paige. But Sammy, Jr.'s amazing tap dancing and hilariously dead-on impersonations of Frank Sinatra, Humphrey Bogart and Louis Armstrong had the celebrity audience cheering him on for "More! More!" The morning papers trumpeted the bravura upstaging (Davis has "hit town" and "set the place on its ear," one critic wrote), and my uncle promptly reversed the marquee: Janis Paige was opening for "The Will Mastin Trio *Featuring Sammy Davis, Jr.*" "I was friends with Sammy for many, many years," Army says.

Scoop-wrangling in Hollywood's golden days was not for the faint of heart. Army drove to Susan Hayward's house to see if she had really been beaten up by her husband, Jess Barker (yep, she had been); he drove to MGM and asked to inspect Judy Garland's wrists ("I was a kid, so nothing fazed me") to see if she'd tried to slit them. (Actually, she hadn't. But let us pause for a moment and imagine a kid journalist today gaining the right to inspect a superstar's allegedly slit wrists.) Still, there were allowances given that wouldn't be today: All the reporters knew that the reason Clark Gable made frequent family-friend visits to Loretta Young and her adopted daughter was that Gable was the father (and Young was the natural, not adoptive, mother), but no one broke the news of Gable's visits or Young's maternal secret.

Moving to *Variety* in 1953, Army built a source library, which he uses to this day. Studio executives', movie stars', publicists'—even ex-presidents'—private phone numbers and addresses are neatly recorded on yellowing, three-by-five cards tucked in 15 cardboard trays. Thumbing through the trays, I am awed: There's barely an unfamous name. Every Friday, Army does an "archive" column, bringing his readers up-to-date on legendary stars. "I spoke to Kim Novak the other day," he says. "How many people can say they spoke to Kim Novak? Oh, and that voice...." His wistful tone makes one recall the sexy alto in *Vertigo*—and imagine how the decades of her silence have only heightened its mystique.

Has he had close calls? Yes! Selma: "You're all ready to report a divorce and the couple are dining together the next night." Times when he couldn't fill his column? Again: Yes! Army: "I've sweated it. I just keep scurrying, making calls" until he gets those 30 items. (Army averages 40 calls a day. And though he successfully transitioned to computer when *Variety* changed over, he, a master of the intimate phone call, still won't use e-mail for his delicate questioning.) Has Selma given Army items? Yes, again. When, in the early 1970s, a broker friend bragged to Selma that she'd just shown Ali MacGraw a Malibu house, "I knew instantly to tell Army." Army read the tea leaves: MacGraw was leaving her husband, Bob Evans, embarking on her love affair with Steve McQueen.

While Army's making his phone calls at the *Variety* office (he still goes in almost every weekday), Selma waxes on about their magical life: George Clooney (the only male star with matinee idol power, she opines) always corners Army at parties. Michael Douglas and Catherine Zeta-Jones ("madly in love with each other") are their friends. They visited Katharine Hepburn in her New York townhouse just before her death, and her living room was crammed, floor to ceiling, with framed images of her, lovingly sent by world-famous painters and photographers. She tells a harrowing-funny story of how Army rushed to George Burns's house upon hearing the iconic comic had died, was ushered up to the bedroom—and left alone with Burns's body. And a hilarious one of Warren Beatty finally making good on years of "Let's have dinner!" promises by taking

Selma and Army to "the most depressing, dark, empty Moroccan restaurant — I wanted to go to Spago, where everyone could see me! — and then talking, and talking, and *talking, stentorianly*, about politics all night." Only to the seen-everything Archerds could an evening with Warren Beatty be, as she puts it, "painful." (Perhaps it was a sneaky kind of punishment for Army's having broken the news of his marriage to Bening.)

Selma remembers the shock of Natalie Wood's drowning death and the utter sadness of her funeral, with Robert Wagner palpably grieving but acting, as always, "gallant." She remembers the anger Merle Oberon leveled on her and Army when they appeared at her Mexico house for dinner not only fashionably late (the other guests had implored them thus) but without the young man that the ageless temptress had requested they find and bring along. Then Selma puts on a DVD of Julie Andrews singing to Army, at a 2003 tribute to him (there was also one in 1993). Andrews calculates that Army has written "9,360,000" words about the industry, all of them "beyond compare, above reproach, and unerringly heartfelt and decent." She then launches into a version of "I've Grown Accustomed to Your Face," singing — in her unmistakable voice — the words as: "We've grown accustomed to his space ... each time we open up the trades ... we just can't wait to hear him say, 'Good morning' every day. His whos, his whats, his dot dot dots...." The camera pans to Army, tearing up in gratitude; then segues to a collage, to the tune of Garland's "Over the Rainbow," of Army with just about every major star of the last 50 years: Marilyn, Cary, Audrey, Dean, Lucille, Marlon, Kirk, Barbra, Bing, Tom Hanks, Tom Cruise, Eddie Murphy, Paul Newman....

"Isn't that touching? Isn't that beautiful?" Selma says, dabbing her eyes. It is touching, immensely so. And so is Selma's love for her husband. And then, of course, she calls him at the office. He's in the middle of his hours of calls to foment column items. Maybe he'll write about the dinner he and Selma just had at Sam Goldwyn's house, where Olivia de Havilland was — at age 92! — "as charming as ever and as smartly attired as ever," Army says. The grand old days are over *only* for those who *let* them be. Both elegant, tireless Archerds know this. They also know about devotion. When he hears Selma's voice, he says, in his soft, careworn voice, "I'm so glad that it's you." ≈

THE GOOD DOCTOR

by DENIS HAMILL

illustrations by BRETT RYDER

I N THE CLINIC, THE OLD DOCTOR SMILES.

He claps a reassuring hand on the young patient's shoulder and listens to his heart with a stethoscope, nodding his full head of silvery hair, taking a penlight out of the breast pocket of his starched white smock bearing the embroidered name: Dr. William Don Putnam, M.D.

The young man has vertigo. His balance is off. His nose runs. His overbooked family doctor can't see him for at least five days. So he's come here, to the Urgent Care After Hours Medical Clinic in the West Valley of Salt Lake City, to see any medicine man who will treat walk-ins off the street.

Dr. Putnam gazes into the young man's right ear. Nods. He knew the answer before he looked. Inner ear infection. He writes a prescription for antibiotics and tells the patient to follow up with the scheduled visit to his family doc.

"But make sure you take every single pill even after you feel better, okay?" he says.

The young man promises and pays his fee to the receptionist, who calls the next patient.

And Dr. Putnam smiles....

....

At home, he used to smile even more.

That was back when Doris was still alive. But ever since, Dr. William Putnam rises each morning about seven, alone here in his spacious, fastidious, two-bedroom $1,000-a-month apartment in Salt Lake's drowsy Old Farm District, a Steve Martini novel bookmarked on his night table, surrounded by snow-buttered Wasatch Mountains, and after injecting himself with insulin for his type 2 diabetes, he showers, dresses in khaki pants, a checkered shirt and soft-soled shoes, pours a single cup of coffee with milk and sugar, switches on the TV to the business news on CNBC, and sits down and pulls on his large-framed glasses to read the *Salt Lake Tribune*.

No longer a strict vegetarian Seventh-Day Adventist, he'll work on the Saturday Sabbath if duty calls and, on doctor's orders (his own), eat a ham-and-cheese omelet with bacon and a hillock of berries with a tall glass of orange juice. At night, he even likes a glass of no-no merlot with his favorite meal of chicken-fried steak.

Oddly, when he glances up at the chiming grandmother clock that he bought with his wife, Dorrie, 44 years and some 385,000 hourly Big Ben chimes ago, right after they married in Tulsa, he even misses the smell of those morning cigarettes that would eventually help kill her.

Dorrie died nine years ago.

And so on most mornings here alone, he stares at the framed watercolors of the Louisiana bayou and the New Orleans French Quarter painted by a barber named

Fruget that he bought on vacation with Dorrie and listens to the soft chimes of the big clock and sees those vanished moments trapped between tick and tock that only he ever gets to see.

And he wishes he was reading the *LA Times*, his favorite newspaper, which he used to share at the kitchen table with Doris through the 1980s when he directed a family residency program at Glendale Adventist Medical Center, in Glendale, California. Those were the best years of his life, when he loved teaching medicine and Dorrie was still healthy, and his three kids were young, and so was he. Sort of. Sure, he could still read the *LA Times* online. In his ninth decade, he's fully computer-literate and keeps up with his professional cyber-obligations. But he's a tad old-fashioned, still listens to Henry Mancini, loves revival musical theater and Indiana Jones movies and chick-flick romantic comedies like *Sleepless in Seattle*, and anything starring Tom Hanks. It makes perfect sense that he learned the most about life and people as a door-to-door salesman across the level American playing fields of Iowa, Oklahoma and "Missourah," and so Dr. William Don Putnam prefers the tactile feel of his morning newspaper, heavy with bad news, in his firm and healing hands.

"A family doc needs to look a patient in the eye," he says, flashing that smile as wide as the delft blue western sky outside his window. His beaming smile, so calming it should require FDA approval, is so distinct that back in the 1980s, on the back of Dr. Putnam's medical ID badge at Verdugo Hills Hospital under IDENTIFYING CHARACTERISTICS, it read: "Engaging, pleasant smile."

"You learn a lot about a patient by looking him in the eye and smiling, putting him at ease and just really listening to him," Dr. Putnam says.

Smiling.

....

In the clinic, later, the old doctor smiles at a boy of 11 suffering from pink eye. Dr. Putnam winks and asks a medical assistant to give the boy an eye exam.

"I can just tell by the angle he looked at me from that this kid needs glasses,"
he says.

The eye test will reveal the boy's vision is 30/70. Dr. Putnam smiles.

"He's been rubbing his eyes because he's seeing blurry," he says. "Might've infected
it. Who knows? He needs two prescriptions. One from me for the infection. One from
an eye doctor for glasses. I'll recommend an eye doctor. He'll be fine. In fact, he'll come
out of this seeing the world a whole lot better. And it can still be a beautiful place…."

Dr. Putnam, with the energy and passion of a man 30 years younger than his 80
birthdays, will keep smiling from 3 p.m. to 10:20 p.m., 20 minutes longer than his
scheduled seven-hour shift, while treating 35 patients in need of urgent "family doc"–
style medical care.

....

Earlier, over breakfast, Putnam talked freely about his life as a family man and
family doctor, smiling into the eyes of tens of thousands of patients in the 54 years since
graduating Loma Linda University medical school in 1954. The son of a banker father
he adored—a man who left the family farm in Deep River, Iowa, a town so small that
"they had one sign that said you were entering and also leaving," to attend Kansas City
Business College—and a devout Adventist mother, young Billy Putnam always knew
he would be a doctor.

"I was born in Flower Hospital in Tulsa, Oklahoma, on December 23, 1927, and
I can't remember a time when I didn't want to be a doctor, but don't ask me why," he
says, staring at the big strawberry at the end of his fork. "I suppose it had to do with
my mom, who raised me as an Adventist. Being a Christian boy who observed the
Sabbath on a Saturday, like Jewish folks, was kinda hard. But I loved my mom, and
all Adventists aspire to careers where they can serve mankind either in the ministry,
medicine, missionary work or education. After I graduated Union College, in Lincoln,
Nebraska, an Adventist school, my grades weren't competitive enough to get into

medical school. So I taught in Iowa for a year and the next year I was accepted into Loma Linda University medical school."

After med school and two years in the air force, Dr. William Don Putnam hung out his M.D. shingle with an associate named Dr. Charlie Wilbanks on Lewis Street in north Tulsa.

First, he did no harm.

Then Dr. Putnam started a career of doing endless good, delivering babies like an assembly-line worker. "Delivering babies is the comedy club of medicine," he says with a hearty laugh, igniting his Anglo-German face in such a way that you can still see the imprint of a happy boyhood beneath the crinkled years.

Scattered around the country today are the adult incarnations of some 4,000 babies Dr. Putnam delivered between 1955 and 1977 at Sewart Air Force Base and in the maternity wards of Tulsa.

In Tulsa, he also raised three children with his first wife, whom he divorced in 1963, the same year his father took sick. His dying father's nurse in the cardiac unit of Hillcrest Hospital in Tulsa was named Doris, and Dr. Putnam would marry her the following year.

"My ex-wife remarried as well, and we remained in the same town and were cordial," says Dr. Putnam. "My kids, John, Cathey and Vicky, all three years apart, were always in my life. I love 'em all to death."

And Dorrie had a 12-year-old daughter named Anne, from a previous marriage, who was congenitally deaf. "She won the very first Miss Deaf America Pageant and today is a teacher in Wisconsin," he says.

John, 53, is an orthopedic surgeon in Springfield, Missouri; Cathey, 50, is an emergency room doctor in Salt Lake; and Vicky, 47, is an intensive-care step-down registered nurse in Boulder, Colorado.

Two years ago, Dr. Putnam moved to Salt Lake from Los Angeles to be closer to Cathey. "I love being near her and the grandkids," he says. "But I also save about

$25,000 a year in insurance, rent and general cost of living here. When I applied for a job at After Hours Medical, I told them they should take my age into consideration. They did. They liked my experience. They hired me."

....

In the clinic, after the sun goes down, Dr. Putnam continues to smile while treating a stream of patients suffering from summer flu, back pain, open wounds.

"I was never an OB," Dr. Putnam says. "I was a family doc. People came to me for everything from a bellyache to tonsillitis to pregnancy. But I have this habit I learned from my father of finishing whatever I start. So if a patient went into labor, I naturally stayed with her in the hospital until the baby was born."

....

Over breakfast, Dr. Putnam says he understands women.

He got to know them best door-to-door to supplement his college tuition. "Going door-to-door selling Christian children's books made me a better doctor," he says. "It made me get to know and really like people. It taught me about rejection and perseverance, and to rise to a challenge. It taught me how hard people worked for a dollar. I learned that if the woman of the house said no right away, I would definitely make a sale. Because it was a challenge. Be honest, be polite, tell the truth, and they'll trust you. Once a woman trusts you, she'll buy from you. Of course, some bought from me just to get rid of me because I was a pain…."

Mostly, women liked Dr. Putnam.

And he knew that pregnant women liked to talk amongst themselves and compare notes. After opening his practice, word spread on the baby-making tom-toms of Tulsa that Dr. Putnam was a doctor with a great bedside manner who stayed with you, smiling and reassuring, from first contraction to the glorious first smack on your baby's behind. Soon women with swollen bellies waddled from all over town to have their babies with Dr. Putnam. "I wasn't a pediatrician either," he says. "But then the moms started bringing their babies to me for postnatal care. And I'd become the mom's doc, too. And the new mom's mom's doc. And pretty soon I'd have had four generations of the same family sitting in my waiting room."

Walking to his car, decades later, Dr. Putnam says he will never forget his very first baby, whom he delivered in his junior year of medical school.

"It was in L.A. County Hospital," he remembers, climbing into his silver 2004 Toyota Camry to drive to work at the clinic. "And the older docs were laughing at me, saying, when she starts shouting … I'd know the baby was coming. So start pushing." He turns the key in the ignition, bringing the car to life, gliding out of the space onto the spotless surface roads of the city known as the Crossroads of the West. "Well, sure enough, she started yelling … And I started pushing! And she pushed back! And it was like pushing against a linebacker! I did all I could to slow it up so the baby didn't drop onto the floor! I couldn't believe her strength or my eyes when that beautiful child came out into the world! It was quite a thrill. Made me fall in love with OB."

Dr. Putnam smiles, his foot pressing on the accelerator like a kid with his first license, whooping onto a highway at 70 mph.

He glances in the rearview, and says, "The interesting thing was that through the years, not everyone liked me. But it sorted itself out. Pretty soon, you looked up, and you had a set of patients that were really yours. You didn't have arguments and problems and lawsuits with patients. You had relationships. I was their family doc, and people came to me for everything under the sun."

....

In the clinic, Dr. Putnam treats a man with a swollen right hand, marching him into the back room for an X-ray. A few minutes later, he's studying the film on a wall-mounted light box, pointing to the fracture.

"We need to get you to a hand specialist," he says, prescribing anti-inflammatory painkillers as a medical assistant calls around to make an appointment for the special hand doctor.

"Pretty soon you looked up, and you had a set of patients that were really yours.

You didn't have arguments and problems and lawsuits with patients. You had relationships."

"You get a different type of patient every 15 minutes," he says, filling out the medical forms in longhand in his small cubbyhole office. "No two patients are alike. It's what keeps life interesting. The biggest misconception is that all docs become rich. Surgeons might. Not family docs. We live comfortably. No complaints. But we have no pension plan. I have Social Security and an IRA but I need to keep working to live comfortably. And I have to save for my old age...."

But it's clear he keeps working for other intrinsic reasons that he doesn't verbalize. Instead, he gives a sly smile as he continues his daily paperwork.

....

But in the car, when he has quiet time to reflect, he reveals that it hasn't been all smiles and laughter and newborn babies.

He often thinks of the 18-year-old son of the family he'd delivered a baby for in Tulsa in the late 1960s. This case would later lead Dr. Putnam to require his family medicine students to work closely with psychologists and social workers when he taught medicine in Glendale.

The kid named Mark came to Dr. Putnam's office one afternoon complaining of a lingering sore throat. As he drives to the clinic to help new patients, Dr. Putnam remembers across the decades that he gave Mark his trademark smile, and looked down his throat with his penlight. There was no redness. No swelling. No infected tonsils. No fever. Putnam had a jam-packed waiting room, and he gently asked the fidgety teen what was really wrong. The squirming kid was eager to talk and said he had some problems he really needed to discuss. But the kid kept glancing at the crying babies and wheezing elderly in the waiting room. "'Don't mind them,' I said," Putnam recalls as if referring to his office notes, the Toyota spinning through Salt Lake.

But the boy just couldn't verbalize his problem. He was fretful. Abashed. Uncomfortable in his own skin. Putnam asked Mark if he'd like to come back the next day before visiting hours. The kid nodded, said he'd like to do that, and left without another word.

"The next morning I was having my coffee and opened my newspaper and saw a story that said that Mark had committed suicide the night before," he said. "I took it hard. I've never forgotten that. Never will. If I had been better trained in psychology, as all family docs should be but aren't, that boy might be alive today. It was a different time. If I can complain about one major thing about modern medicine, it is that we've lost the personal relationship. I think most of the mistakes I've ever made with patients came from not having enough time to talk to them. I sure wish I hadn't let that kid walk out of my office that day. I wish I had demanded Mark stay and talk to me."

He stares off into the crumpled mountains, the car decelerating, his smile in full retreat, replaced with a grimace of nagging regret.

In this fragile moment, this perfect gentleman who personifies the phrase "good doctor" looks like he needed to tell that story as badly as did the kid named Mark, who never got to tell his.

The doctor's unforgiving reverie is broken when asked about his most memorable baby delivery. He recalls a pregnant woman to whom he had given a saddle block anesthesia in the delivery room, and who was wide awake during delivery. "And she looked up at me after her beautiful little baby girl was born and said, 'You just had a little baby girl yourself, didn't ya?' I said, yeah, that my wife had given birth to a baby girl named Cathey Ann three days before. The woman asked, 'Do you mind if I call my baby Cathey Ann, too?' I said I'd be flattered. And so somewhere out in Tulsa I guess there's a Cathey Ann, three days younger than my Cathey Ann."

The Toyota picks up speed again, zipping into the West Valley of Salt Lake, once considered the wrong side of the tracks but now going through a surge of new development.

There are patients here who need him.

....

In the clinic, Dr. Putnam treats a middle-aged man for a sore throat. That's easy. But he doesn't like the man's pallor. He asks if he has indigestion. The man says yes.

He knows that's the most common symptom of a heart problem. Then he discovers that the man also has high blood pressure. He hooks him to an EKG to read his heart. Not good. Dr. Putnam uses a transient patient's sore throat visit to set the patient up with a proper cardiologist and a family doctor. "It's rewarding just to triage people who don't know they are so close to a catastrophic illness," he says.

He fills out forms and prescriptions, and doesn't join the medical chorus complaining about HMOs and malpractice insurance. "I'm just happy to be working," he says. "Doing what I know best. Making sick people better. But I'll be going out of town for three months come next week to work in Joplin, Missouri, where I'll earn in that time what I make here in six months. Plus I'll be near my son, John, who lives in nearby Springfield. Then I'll be back…."

And then he gets up to treat the next patient….

. . . .

Earlier, in the car, before the clamor of the clinic, he's asked if there was a most memorable patient.

"My wife, Dorrie," he says, without hesitation, his eyes never leaving the road. He says he and Dorrie had a loving marriage in California, where he taught family-practice medicine at the Glendale Adventist Medical Center.

"But I never felt closer to or loved my Doris more than when she was dying," he says. "Do want to know why?" Yes. "Because she needed me. I remember one night near the end, Dorrie was lying in bed, suffering from chronic obstructive lung disorder, hooked to the oxygen tank. Restless. Wheezing. Fitful. Couldn't sleep because of the nicotine withdrawal. There wasn't much I could do to help so I disconnected her oxygen, walked her out of the room, and told her to go ahead and light one of her low-tar-and-nicotine cigarettes. She did. And it soothed her. Calmed her down. After that she could sleep. It gave me great inner comfort that I could make her feel better.

Her needing me made me love her so deeply that it made her death in July 1999 all the worse."

Later, in his apartment, as the grandmother clock tolls, he talks about living alone as a widower for the past nine years.

"I go to the movies alone a lot because I can't get anyone to go with me," he says. "I like to eat Italian, but I don't like dining out alone. I go to my daughter Cathey's quite often for dinner up in the mountains. I keep asking her why she keeps on trying to fix me up with old ladies my age." He laughs. "How about a few in their 60s? Truth is, when you reach my age, most people have too much baggage in their lives, children, grandchildren, great-grandchildren, to make a relationship work."

So he eats a lot of meals alone. At home. Where the grandmother clock he bought with Doris ticks like a second heartbeat.

"Do you want to know when I feel the loneliest?" Yes. "When I'm with my grown children. Do you want to know why?" Yes. "Because after Dorrie died I saw that they were very sad because she was like a surrogate mother and a friend and confidante to them. They loved her. But I saw that they went on with their lives without her just fine. And it suddenly made me realize that although they love me, and I love them, they will also get along without me just fine after I die. Which meant they didn't need me anymore. That's a lonely realization in a man's life...."

That's why, at 80, he continues to work as a doctor, isn't it?

Because that's where he's still needed.

He sits back, the smile igniting his face, and says, "You know, I never thought about that, but you're probably right. My patients really do need me. And so, yeah, I guess I need them, too."

In the car, he pulls into a spot in the strip mall behind the Urgent Care After Hours Medical Clinic, and steps out carrying his crisp white smock. He pulls open the door and enters, passing through the waiting room, crowded with patients who need him. ❧

True Love

....

by JOYCE WADLER

illustrations by RICCARDO VECCHIO

L ET US NOW PRAISE MARK SMITH'S BUTT. NOT FOR ITS FIRMNESS
and muscularity, for the old boy is 81 and recovering from a quadruple bypass; not for
the years it sat planted in a four-wheel-drive vehicle as Smith, godfather of off-road
driving, jolted and bounced on adventures from the jungles of Colombia to the deserts
of Madagascar, but for its tattoo.

It's a simple tattoo, carrying only the name of Smith's true love. He had it done
14 years ago when he was an impetuous lad of 67 and his daughter Jill, the kid who
inherited her father's adventurer spirit and runs the adventure travel company he
started, Jeep Jamboree USA, paid for it as a Father's Day gift. Hundreds by now have
seen it and more; in the early days, lacking the finesse to expose only the salient part,
Smith simply dropped his pants.

The tattoo reads "Jeep," which is what Smith is driving today, a hot weekend in summer, on the winding canyon roads near his home in California's High Sierra.

His destination is a 22-mile mountain roadway called the Rubicon Trail, a course of boulders and ravines so feared and revered in four-wheel-drive circles, where fear and reverence are interchangeable virtues, that its name was given to the fancy, duded-up Jeep Smith is driving now, a vehicle he helped develop for the Jeep company. He doesn't drive fast, even though he's taught extreme off-road driving to the U.S. Army Special Forces and law enforcement people throughout the state of California. His white hair is pulled back in a long ponytail, and he wears a white straw hat with a band decorated with some sort of animal teeth, which makes him look like a latter-day Indian elder. Smith's traveling companion, a large Siberian husky named J.J., has been exiled to the backseat, from which he literally breathes down a visitor's neck.

"Got this hat in Australia," Smith had said at the beginning of the trip. "White hat's kinda become my trademark. Know what these are? Crocodile teeth."

"No kidding. Where'd you get 'em?" one asks, prepared for a Great Adventurer's story.

Smith, his setup neatly executed, laughs: "In a shop."

The two-way mountain road Smith is driving is something more than a series of hairpin turns and switchbacks; it deserves a word of its own, which written would look like this: /\/\/\/\/\. As Smith rounds a bend, a teenage boy on a Japanese motorcycle comes tearing down the road at him.

"Goddamn rice rockets! Sake sippers!" yells Smith, whose rough edges, like those of the mighty Rubicon Trail, have proven impervious to the erosion of time.

What does he have against Japanese bikes?

"Don't have anything against them. You just shouldn't be driving them 100 miles an hour down these roads. Kid came down the road last weekend wrapped himself around a tree. That was his last drive."

Your dog, Mr. Smith, seems to be kind of drooling on my neck, the visitor says.

There is a roar that makes you wonder what Smith was like before the bypass that allegedly slowed him down.

"GODDAMN, J.J.! Get back there!"

Let us turn our thoughts now to True Love, Fated Love, a Brad-and-Angelina sort of love, but you are Brad and the Jeep is Angelina. Mark Smith, whose father is a Nevada mining engineer, sees his first Jeep when he is 12 or 13, in a movie theater, on the *Movietone News*. It's the late 1930s; there are no televisions or computer games; it is his *Raiders of the Lost Ark*, his *Hellboy*, his *Grand Theft Auto*. Years later, as one does with true love, he will remember that first glimpse: It's this boxy little vehicle, no top, it's bouncing across the hills; you do not need to be bound by roads and signs and Rand McNally, you can go anywhere you like.

Smith grows up. He enlists in the marines in World War II. When he gets out, he marries a girl named Irene and buys his first Jeep, army surplus, in the same year, 1951. The newlyweds have desk jobs lined up in Las Vegas, but on their honeymoon, they stop in Georgetown, a tiny logging town an hour east of Sacramento. "God's country," Smith says. They never leave. It is in Georgetown Smith learns of an old Indian trail called the Rubicon that takes you 6,000 feet into the High Sierra, then through to Lake Tahoe. It's no idyllic dirt road wending through the mountains. It's 22 miles of rock on rock, with boulders the height of a truck; if you don't go in with another vehicle and a winch, you're a fool. In 1953, Mr. Smith comes up with an idea to bring a little money into Georgetown: He organizes trips for Jeep owners along the Rubicon Trail, called the Jeepers Jamboree.

Smith does lots of other things over the years. He has four kids, works as deputy sheriff for El Dorado County, builds a little shopping center in Georgetown modeled after a miners' town, buys and sells properties, becomes a rich man.

But it's all secondary to the Jeep adventures: running the Jeepers Jamborees out of Georgetown, starting his own company, Jeep Jamboree USA, which organizes off-road trips around the world. He learns how to handle a Jeep in the most challenging off-road conditions by trial and error, and word gets around. In 1982, after a California deputy rolls her car in a mountain chase, the Los Angeles County Sheriff's Department brings Smith in to teach off-road driving in hazardous terrain. He opens the course, which his company still gives, to all law enforcement officers—even the Canadian Mounties attend. Smith becomes a paid consultant to Jeep, helping build what he estimates to be 100 off-track courses for Jeep dealers across the country. He teaches Special Forces and the marines. He is never injured, never even rolls a vehicle, although one time, when he's sitting alongside a panicked journalist (as he takes care to note, a woman journalist), he is in a Jeep that rolls.

The biggest adventure, the one that makes Mark Smith famous in off-road circles, is the 1978–1979 Expedición de las Americas, in which he leads a group of off-roaders on a 120-day, 20,000-mile journey from the tip of Tierra del Fuego, in South America, to Prudhoe Bay, Alaska. The most dangerous part of the journey is a stretch called the Darién Gap, 250 miles of jungle and swamp between Panama and Colombia, in which expedition members (actually the locals they hire) hack their way through the jungle.

What made him want to do this trip?

"The challenge," Smith says. "It was like a great big boil on your butt, it's irritating. Different groups tried it. The British army did cross it, I think, in 1972. They took 250 men; it took them 100 days just to do the jungle portion. They had so many men they coulda carried the goddamn vehicles. They lost eight Colombian marines in a river crossing. We did the same thing in 30 days with 16 North Americans and 25 Indians cutting trail. They were not four-wheel-drive people. It was like taking a bunch of bicycles to Mount Everest."

The memories this trip inspires as Mark Smith drives toward the Rubicon Trail on a hot summer day: ants the size of a silver dollar! Hoof-and-mouth disease to the north, bandits to the south! Snakes! The expedition fords mountain crevices with custom steel ladders and inches Jeeps up 60-degree slopes. One day, it takes them nine hours to go 600 feet. The experts had said no man over 40 could survive the trip. Smith was 51. Driving the Darién Gap, his foot became so infected from red mite bites — "they have a little tube they insert into your flesh to draw the fluid out, and if you scratch, that little tube can get stuck there" — the doctor wanted to airlift him out. No way, Smith said, it was his expedition; he would have shot them if they tried.

The road rounds a bend and suddenly opens on Loon Lake, a lake in a blue vodka ad, clean as ice. On the road, and on the shoulders of the road, are dozens of RVs, each one taller, beefier and emblazoned with more road-warrior doodads than the next. The road skirts the lake, then turns left and stops at what appears to be a hill of rock, spotted with fir and boulders: the Rubicon Trail.

Millions of words have been written in women's magazines in an attempt to answer one of the great modern mysteries: Where have all the men gone? They are here in their four-wheel hulks, on the Rubicon Trail, as the temperature approaches 100 degrees: happily hung up on rocks, towing one another with elaborate winches and pulleys, pulling on cans of fortifying liquids, gathering about one another and encouraging each other on under gathering layers of dust/sweat/oil/grit. And who was it brought this all to being? The cranky old guy with the tattoo on his butt.

Smith, after a dismissive look at one or two incompetents, parks his Jeep on the hill and scans the skies for a helicopter pilot he knows. He uses "heel-a-copters," as he calls them, to bring in supplies for his trips. His camp at Rubicon Springs is only 12 miles in—it's a beautiful spot—but driving there would take eight or nine hours. The heel-a-copter could get there in 20 minutes. Hearing that the visitor has never been in a heel-a-copter makes Mr. Smith all the more excited. The pilot's a real nice guy, he says. Just got his license.

The visitor is less enthused. Earlier in the day at the Jeep Jamboree USA offices, when she had met Smith's daughter Jill and her husband, Pearse Umlauf, the company general manager, and was presented with the company T-shirt with a photo of Smith's tattooed butt ("Thank you. So this is, like, the official shirt?"), Jill had been talking about this very helicopter ride. It had been fantastic, she'd said. They'd gone swooping up the mountains and dropping down into canyons; you had this feeling that if you died, it would be a great way to go.

Now the visitor envisions a shattered helicopter and bodies mangled beyond recognition. A California trooper who has taken Smith's off-road driving course will spot a plump fragment of skin and flesh, with the letters J E E P.

"Hey, wait a minute," he'll say. "I know that butt."

With no helicopter in sight, Smith drives a little of the Rubicon Trail. He noses the Jeep over rocks two and three feet high, slowly trickling over the other side. What's important is to make sure your wheel is on the tallest part of the rock, he says. Otherwise you're going to get hung up…. Naah, it doesn't hurt the underside of your vehicle. It's good for it. Keeps the rust off. Anyway, there's a plate on the bottom.

Smith drives the Jeep back to the crest of the rock and parks. He spots the pilot's Jeep, goes over, and opens the back to an ice freezer and helps himself to two cold bottles of water, one for the writer, one for himself and the dog, and then returns to his own vehicle.

"Here you go, ho-neee," he says to the dog, pouring the water in a bowl.

One or two of the men, subscribers, no doubt, to *Off-Road* magazine, have spotted Mr. Smith and are sneaking looks, the way you do when you spot a celebrity. Another young man walks over to the Jeep and greets Smith respectfully by name.

"I don't know who the hell that is," Smith says after he leaves.

He sits in the Jeep, feeling the heat despite the air conditioning, keeping a lookout for the helicopter. This reminds him of a story. Years ago, he and Irene and Jill are in New York, at a piano bar at the St. Moritz, and there's a piano player in a tux with a candelabra on the piano. Smith says that's just what he needs for the Rubicon. They tell him he's crazy, which is, to Smith, as the starting gun was to Secretariat. Back in California, Smith finds a piano rental guy in Reno who says he'll rent him a piano and let him airlift it 20 miles over the mountains, as long as he gets a picture—he'll put it in a newspaper ad that says "We deliver anywhere." As Smith is standing in the woods, waiting, a ranger comes along and says he's heard the craziest thing: Smith is planning to airlift in a grand piano. "You're right, that is crazy," Smith says. A few minutes later, here comes the piano, dangling from the chopper.

Smith's heel-a-copter, on the other hand, is happily nowhere in sight, and with the sun beating down and Mr. Smith's recent medical adventure, it's decided it's time to head for home.

Given the pilot's lack of experience, the visitor admits to Smith that she is not unhappy to miss this ride. This prompts an admission of his own from Smith: The pilot has actually flown for American Airlines for years. Chuckling, snuggled up close to his true love, Smith turns back onto the road and heads down the mountain for home. ❧

✤

The Greatest of Ease

by DAVID EVANIER

illustrations by PIETARI POSTI

Hugo, oklahoma, is a circus town, the winter home to several traveling circuses, and Grace McIntosh McFarland, a former trapeze artist, is, at 93, its oldest celebrity. Some performers, like Grace, retire to Hugo, and many more rest permanently in the "Showmen's Rest" section of Mount Olivet Cemetery near the center of town. Grace is a frequent visitor.

As she walks swiftly among the graves, birds chirping above, the atmosphere is anything but somber. Here, carved elephants strike jaunty poses on their stone perches. Showpeople in full regalia and high hats, flamenco fan dancers, clowns, and kids holding

balloons prance in bas-relief. A likeness of the Great Huberto walks the tightrope, with an umbrella, for eternity. Terry Fenne, the Mud Show Elephant Man, has a little bench that invites visitors to *have a seat on me*. Looking less like a grave marker and more like a permanent marquee, another tombstone proclaims: *We gave the world a smile each day*.

Grace McFarland gave plenty of smiles to the world during her 40 years as an entertainer. For more than two decades, she performed an aerial act with the best-known circuses of the day—among them Clyde Beatty, Ringling Brothers, James M. Cole, Shrine and Tom Mix. Then, when she felt herself pass her peak strength in her early 50s, she climbed down off the rigging to start a show of her own. Never mind that she lacked a business degree, or much formal education at all, or that she worked at a time—and in a business—when few women called the shots. She defied the conventions of the day, running the small but well-regarded M & M International Circus for nearly 30 years before retiring to Hugo in 1991.

During one of her regular visits to Showmen's Rest, she talks about just how lucky she's been. "I've had a long run—and a good run," she says, referring to her show-stopping act. But later, reflecting on the accomplishments she values most, Grace dwells on the more quotidian pleasures: love and devotion to her adopted family, two solid marriages, the opportunity to raise her first husband's niece, her deep faith, the respect of her community and the affection of the handful of younger friends she holds close. "I've been very blessed."

Grace's friends say the blessing goes both ways. "Everyone loves her," says Donna Galvano. "She's a very caring person." Five years ago, a stroke left Grace almost totally deaf. Donna, a bookkeeper for one of the local circus troupes, began helping Grace manage phone calls. These days, they're close friends, and Donna hosts Grace for brunch at her home every Sunday.

Margaret, a waitress at the popular Angie's Circus Cafe, says that even in a town of fire-breathers, jugglers and lion tamers, Grace stands out as something special. "We all love her," she says. "She gets really down over her deafness. But she still manages to always overcome those moods. She loves life."

It's been nearly half a century since Grace stood on the back of a white stallion wearing a silver-sequined leotard, a billowing cape and a feathered headdress over her short, curly brown hair. That hair is gray now, and time has loosened her well-defined muscles. Still, little flourishes of her exotic life remain. Not long ago, she greeted a visitor wearing plain slacks, an unadorned short-sleeved shirt, white ankle socks and — surprise — a pair of white, Chinese-style slippers embroidered with two bright red alligators. Grace dismisses the notion that she's anything but ordinary. She was, she says, more than anything else, a circus professional. It's hard for the rest of the world to grasp, she knows, but the seesawing notes of the circus pipe organ, the acrid smell of elephant dung over the dusty smell of fresh hay, the ability to swing through the still, cool air far above the heads of a gaping crowd — it was all in a day's work to Grace. "It was just what we did," she says.

Unlike so many who make their living under the Big Top, Grace wasn't born into the circus life. For 14 years, she lived in a working-class section of then-bustling Detroit. Her mother had died when she was a baby, and her father remarried twice. Grace didn't get along well with either stepmother. "They weren't mean to me," she says. "But there was no love there."

With upheaval at home and under pressure from his wife, Grace's father sent her to live with another family, the Romigs, when she was 14. At that moment, her life took a turn straight out of a child's storybook. "My foster mother was a bareback rider. My father was a wirewalker. My brother was a clown," Grace says. Instead of attending the local high school, she learned to be a performer. "My folks trained me. They taught me trapeze. My father taught me rodeo. I did dressage: I would sit on the horse and the horse dances. Then the horse would lie down and sit up while I was in the saddle. I did trick rides. I did everything. My finish was something called muscle grinds on the trapeze—revolving around the bar doing different tricks. It took a lot of muscle to do them. I put towels on my arms when I first practiced and learned to do them. My foster dad put the rigging up for me so it was safe."

Working in a circus meant the Romigs and their foster daughter were traveling across America almost constantly—and without the opportunity to put down roots or develop friendships outside the family. Grace became quickly and permanently devoted to the Romigs. For 15 years, they depended on each other for everything—for love, companionship and their livelihood. "The Romigs, my foster parents, were very good to me. They never bought anything for their kids they didn't buy for me, too. I loved my foster mother," she recalls. So much so that Grace postponed marriage until she was 29 — late for an attractive woman in that era. She preferred to be the Romigs' daughter, she says, more than a husband's wife.

In yellowed photos from the early days of her career, Grace broadcasts an indelible air of confidence. She is kneeling on a horse with a pompom on its forelock. She is wearing a one-piece capri-legged leotard, a saucy bow tie and a waist-length cape. She is holding a riding crop, but it's clear from her triumphant smile that the crop is more prop than tool. The horse — and everyone under the Big Top that day — knew exactly who was in charge.

She was even more self-assured on the trapeze. A 1947 program describes her as "a dainty little lady, the most sensational and daring aerialist ever presented beneath the Big Top... pulchritude and plethoric plenitude... everything seems to stop as Grace dallies with death in the dome of the big tent."

Her poise caught the eye of the casting director for Cecil B. DeMille's famous spectacle *The Greatest Show on Earth*. She's in two scenes of that movie. In one, she performs on the velvet-covered rope called "the web," which hangs from the top of the Big Top to the dirt floor. In another, as a fill-in for a cast member who was injured, she wears a Hawaiian grass skirt and dances a hula on the tightrope while Dorothy

Lamour sings. "The producer said, 'Oh, Grace can do it. She can do anything,'" recalls Grace. Some years later, she also appeared on *The Ed Sullivan Show*.

It wasn't all rousing applause and brushes with fame. Bad things happened, too. In her career as a performer, Grace had two breathtaking plunges. One came after she made a bet about how many times she could spin around a bar on her forearms. She got up to 300 and then tumbled. "I let go of the thing and that was it. I went headfirst that way, like 35 feet," she says. Her foster father caught her. "I fell in his arms. I landed on the back of my head. It didn't knock me out. He said, 'That's what you get when you get a big head.' That was enough to straighten me out. I was about 17, a smart-aleck kid."

Her second fall, in Calumet, Michigan, was more frightening. "I went off the flyboard where they catch the trapeze," she says, "and I landed in the net. It took my breath away. That had never happened before." Her injury was unsightly but not life-threatening. "My face was so big on one side, I could see it with my other eye. But I was always fortunate, really."

Spectators stare agog when they watch the trapeze acts, instinctively reacting to the primal fear of great heights that is programmed into the DNA of most mortals. But when Grace was working, fear wasn't something she had to master. "I didn't think about anything but the work. I thought about doing it right, pointing my toes, everything that I was taught. You do a job. You go in, two shows a day, there's no excitement in that." Gratitude, she says, filled the hole where fear might otherwise have blossomed. "I loved the circus. I always felt lucky to be doing it." Faith helped, too: Grace is a fervent Roman Catholic. Even now, "Saying the rosary is the most important part of my day. I'm not crazy religious, but I think you should be thankful for things."

After McFarland quit performing, helped raise a daughter, built and eventually stopped producing the M & M International Circus, she moved to Hugo. In retirement, she married her second husband, Walter, only to lose him 10 years later to cancer. She also became an avid volunteer, first at the Special Olympics and, later, at the Choctaw Memorial Hospital in her community, where she visited patients for 11 years, hoping to relieve, if just for a moment, their boredom and trepidation. She's given that up lately but still tries her best to entertain the visiting nurses who come by regularly to check on her and take her blood pressure.

Back at Showmen's Rest in the Mount Olivet Cemetery, Grace is looking for one particular tombstone. As she walks among the circus statuary, she reflects on her life as a performer. "I miss the circus. I loved it. All I can say is I had a great life. I don't think anybody had a better life." Her eyes brim. "Wherever I worked, even the shopping centers and the churches, I did everything to the best of my ability. I loved every minute."

At last, she finds what she is seeking—a carved stone marker with an image of Grace on the trapeze. "This is mine," she says, ever the stage manager, firmly in control to the very end. "I had it made up before. I have all my funeral arrangements made." Her birth date reads July 15, 1915. "Holy cow," she says, laughing. "I'm old."≈

MAN AND MACHINE

....

by DAVID KOCIENIEWSKI
illustrations by CHRIS SILAS NEAL

EVEN AT THE TENDER AGE OF 10, RICHARD ZAMBONI COULD SENSE
something fateful under way whenever he spied his father wielding the welder's chalk.

Most of the time, to most people, Frank Zamboni appeared like millions of other
American dads trying to raise a family in the shadow of World War II. But when
he wasn't tending to his son and two daughters or running his refrigeration business,
Frank was also a restless inventor, driven by the idea that you could always make
something better.

So when he used some leftover parts from ice-making equipment to create an open-
air skating rink, Frank Zamboni's success presented him with a new problem: So many
skaters flocked to the arena that the ice needed frequent resurfacing, but grooming the

rink was such a time-consuming ordeal that most customers left long before it ended. Solving that dilemma became a crusade, and Frank spent whatever spare moments he could muster in back of the ice rink—surrounded by compressors, engines and acetylene torches, shirtsleeves rolled up, cigarette dangling from his mouth—searching for inspiration.

"You would see him back there, and sometimes he'd get some sort of insight and pick up a piece of the chalk his welder used and draw the plans out right there on the floor," recalls Richard, now 76. "I was just a kid and didn't know what it all meant. But I could tell it was something important. And I needed to stay out of his way and let him think."

Frank Zamboni's perseverance and ingenuity paid off, revolutionizing the way ice rinks around the world operated, and creating an enduring cultural icon along the way. The chunky machine with the lilting name not only became as indispensable to skaters as blades, laces and hot chocolate, it also attracted the kind of cult following that has seen it celebrated everywhere from heavy-metal songs to "Peanuts" comic strips. And the Zamboni family business, which Richard still serves as president, has flourished, and today is more closely identified with its product than anything this side of the Jacuzzi.

"I was at a convention a few years ago and told a woman my name," Richard says. "And she said 'Right—and my name's Julius Caesar!'"

Given the frosty nature of the family legacy, it's tempting to assume that the Zambonis trudged out of the fjords of Norway, or the elk and dogsled country of northern Ontario. But the legend actually began among the sun and palm trees of southern California, where a 19-year-old Utah native named Frank Zamboni settled on the rural fringe of Los Angeles in 1920.

A born tinkerer, Frank studied to become an electrician and then opened a block-ice company with his brother to serve the Dutch dairy farming community where they lived. As the refrigerator became a fixture in American kitchens, however, it was clear that icemen were headed the way of the buggy whip, so Frank, his brother and a cousin rigged up some spare refrigeration equipment to build Iceland, one of the nation's largest outdoor skating rinks.

But keeping the ice smooth without shooing customers off the rink for long swaths of time was impossible back then, because the best resurfacing technology of the day was part Rube Goldberg, part Currier & Ives. The process began with a large metal planer being dragged by a tractor (or sometimes a man) to scrape off the top layer of ice. Next, a four-man shovel brigade scooped up the snow shavings and hauled them off the rink. Then a barrel of steaming water was rolled around the rink, spreading a layer of water that was evened out with squeegees so it could freeze into a fresh topcoat of ice.

"When they finished, the ice was beautiful," Richard recalls. "And the rink was nearly empty because people grew tired of waiting."

Frank Zamboni needed a solution, and like moonlight inventors in countless American basements, barns and garages, he was determined to devise it himself. It took two years for Zamboni to produce the first prototype, a Ford-Ferguson tractor with a trailer hitched to the back. But when it was tested on the rink in 1942, it failed to smooth the ice or clean up the scrapings.

Zamboni pressed on, but it wasn't until after World War II, when a flood of surplus military parts became available, that he found his breakthrough. Grafting an assortment of components onto a frame that was mounted on axles from a Dodge army truck, Zamboni's fourth prototype finally managed to resurface in one efficient swoop around the rink: a steel plane shaved the ice; a conveyor belt scooped the shavings into a wooden bin mounted on its chassis; and two 67-gallon steel tanks washed the ice, and then spread a new coat of water that quickly froze into a glassy surface.

When the "model A" lumbered onto the rink at Iceland on May 6, 1949, looking like a tractor that had never quite shaken loose its wooden packing crate, patrons weren't sure what to make of the rolling, rattling behemoth. But no one could argue with the results, which allowed skaters to return to the ice in 20 minutes or less!

Zamboni's accomplishment might never have been known outside of Iceland had it not been for Sonja Henie, the Norwegian figure skater who followed her Olympic success by touring with her Hollywood Ice Revue. Practicing at the rink during a stop in Los Angeles, she became so enamored of Zamboni's invention that she pleaded with him to build one she could take on the road. As Henie and the ice show toured the U.S., the resurfacing machine, billed as "The Thing," attracted as much attention as the skaters themselves, and the Zambonis were soon fielding requests from across the country.

But that popularity brought its own challenge: figuring out a way to fill them.

"I was at a conve
years ago and to
my name. And
said 'Right—an
name's Julius C

ntion a few
d a woman
she
d my
aesar."

American history is littered with brilliant ideas that failed as business ventures. Frank Zamboni never intended his machine to be a moneymaking enterprise, and had no experience in manufacturing, so moving the Zamboni vision from the backyard to mass production was nearly as tricky as inventing it.

While the machine might have appeared crude on the outside, it was a marvel of integrated design—difficult to duplicate and complex to operate. It demanded that the driver deftly manage the physics of freezing—regulating the cut of the blade, the humidity, the temperature and flow of the water—all without losing control on the treacherous ice surface and crashing through the boards.

In his effort to make every machine as efficient and user-friendly as possible, Frank Zamboni spent years devising revision after revision. The homemade frame was replaced by a Willys Jeep. The conveyor belt was eventually swapped out for the kind of auger used on snow blowers. The driver's seat was raised, and later a dumping mechanism was added to reduce the time involved in emptying the snow from the tank.

The company finally settled on a standard design in 1954 and, for the first time, produced 20 identical machines. Richard, who had served in the air force and studied business at Loyola University in Los Angeles, was drafted into the family business and, after taking a few courses in mechanical drawing, became responsible for the byzantine process of translating his father's ideas into workable schematic plans.

"My father drove me crazy by constantly changing the design—for years, no two machines were the same," Richard says. "But he wanted to keep making it as effective as possible because his philosophy was simple: 'In the end, what you have to sell is the ice.'"

That credo proved so persuasive that by the end of the 1950s, nearly every team in the National Hockey League was using the machines between periods. In 1960, Zamboni machines made their television debut at the Winter Olympics in Squaw Valley, California, launching the business worldwide.

The Zambonis have sold nearly 9,000 machines since then, in more than 100 countries around the world, even penetrating the Iron Curtain during the Cold War. There are larger models for mammoth rinks in Japan, where speed skaters compete, and in Sweden, where the traditional ice sport of bandy remains popular. The company even produces a small version that hooks onto the back of a lawn tractor for homeowners with backyard ice rinks.

Throughout the years, the mesmerizing sight of the resurfacer slowly circling rinks (typical maximum speed is 9 mph) has made it a kind of cultural phenomenon. Small towns in the North Country use them to lead winter parades, NASCAR drivers like Richard Petty have driven souped-up models, and writers on the sitcom *Cheers* arranged for Carla's second husband, Eddie, to die in a resurface-and-run accident.

Cartoonist Charles Schulz included it in nearly 50 comic strips, including one where Charlie Brown declares, "There are three things in life that people like to stare at: a flowing stream, a crackling fire and a Zamboni clearing the ice."

After the Zambonis ran a prosperous family business for more than 50 years without a whiff of scandal, the Zamboni machine was even dubbed "the last great role model in sport" by *Sports Illustrated* magazine.

Richard Zamboni is so quick to assign credit for the company's success to his late father's creativity, and the machine itself, it would be easy to view him as simply a curator who has preserved and refined the family traditions. But that humility belies a resourcefulness that has allowed him to guide the company through a period of rapid growth and fend off challenges from competitors in North America and Europe (some of whom occasionally ignore the trademark and refer to their products as Zamboni). Richard also has concentrated on building the family brand by licensing a broad line of Zamboni products: T-shirts and license-plate frames, children's books and windup toys, and mock street signs that warn, "Zamboni XING."

Though he has turned over much of the day-to-day operations to his son Frank, who runs the Canadian operation in Brantford, Ontario, Richard occupies his father's former office at the company's factory in Paramount, California, where more than 30 employees still produce machines, and it's not uncommon to see them test-driven on side streets. He's also a familiar presence at Iceland, two blocks away, which the city of Paramount considers a landmark. Although Richard only skates once a year—on Christmas, the only day Iceland is closed, he and three generations of Zambonis take to the ice—Richard stops in frequently to give tours and show off the early models, which are still on display. On occasion, Zamboni will even hop onto the back of a machine and ride along as it cuts the ice, to show off the family namesake at work.

"After all these years, it's basically the same," he said, the engine humming, ice chips ricocheting off his pant leg. "A sharp blade, a conveyor belt and a tank of water." ≈

Excellent and Fair

by COLIN HARRISON

illustrations by RACHEL SALOMON

IT'S EIGHT O'CLOCK ON A SOFT SUNDAY EVENING IN JUNE IN MANHATTAN'S theater district, a time of year when the city surrenders its urgency to the slower pace of summer. Rose Styron has joined her daughters, granddaughters and friends in the back of the restaurant Orso before making her annual journey to Martha's Vineyard for the summer. Tanned and dressed elegantly all in white, she's just seen the most recent revival of *South Pacific*, and it appears the show was most satisfactory; the table is full of conversation, food and good wine.

One is immediately struck by Rose's warmth and intelligence. Not to mention her genuinely dazzling smile, which conveys both good cheer and resilience as she discusses the most difficult chapter of her remarkable life.

When her husband, the celebrated novelist William Styron, died in 2006 at 81, Rose watched as the world remembered his works, which included his first novel, *Lie Down in Darkness; The Confessions of Nat Turner* (winner of the 1967 Pulitzer Prize); and *Sophie's Choice*, a masterful examination of the Holocaust, which became a huge bestseller and displayed William Styron at his full power as a novelist. William, who suffered severe bouts of depression, was revered, too, for his groundbreaking and honest memoir of his illness, *Darkness Visible*. Indeed, many readers first found William Styron through his unflinching memoir. His death, along with those of a handful of other American novelists, signaled the end of a period of post–World War II American letters during which novelists took on large social themes and injected themselves without apology into the broader cultural conversation. American novelists of the era had a kind of societal perch that is more or less unknown today. William Styron was also one of the founders of *The Paris Review*, along with Peter Matthiessen and George Plimpton. James Baldwin and James Jones were part of their ongoing Paris scene.

After William's death, Rose entered the new landscape of widowhood, which, in her case, was a very public one. And this life change was perhaps especially wrenching, as she and her husband had lived an unusually settled life, having resided on the same rural property in Roxbury, Connecticut, for more than 50 years. It was largely on this property that the novelist composed his books, in a small studio across from their house, and where Rose Styron composed their life together. There were three daughters and a son to raise, visiting writers to host, tennis matches to play (Rose remains an active doubles player) and poems to write. And there was Rose's longstanding involvement in a variety of arts and humanitarian endeavors.

Rose Burgunder and William Styron had met briefly in the fall of 1952 at Johns Hopkins University. But they renewed their acquaintance in Rome when William was staying at the American Academy, having won the Prix de Rome for his first novel.

Rose had traveled to Italy to shape her master's thesis into a book. She and William were married that spring.

"Italy was too beautiful," Rose remembers, "too distracting. Bill couldn't work there." So the young couple returned to the United States and moved into an apartment on East 61st Street, but it was difficult to concentrate there, too; the building across the street was being torn down and rebuilt.

Seeking a place more conducive to writing, the couple visited Roxbury, Connecticut, and one Sunday morning went out to look at houses with a real estate agent. They stopped first at a small white pillared home with a charming southern hollyhock garden. The agent rang the bell. No one answered. The agent lifted Rose up to the window because they could hear Lohengrin blaring from a phonograph—"I was lighter and twentysomething," she remembers now. She saw an older couple lying on the floor, martinis in hand. The gentleman, it turned out, was one Rev. Arthur Styron, a cousin of her husband's father, probably the only Styron living north of the Mason-Dixon line and a writer, too. He had been Roxbury's Episcopal minister "defrocked for drinking," Rose theorized. A small world.

"Then we went around a country corner and saw another house and we loved it, a big old dilapidated place with a barn and a guesthouse."

The property had once been occupied by Russian aristocrats who'd gone into exile in 1917, and came complete with outbuildings and musty old Russian medical texts. The Styrons bought the place in 1954, and it would become not just the location where William "wrote best," Rose says—wrote some of the greatest American novels of the second half of the 20th century, it might be added—but where they raised their four children, as Roxbury meanwhile became an artists' community. Arthur Miller and Alexander Calder lived just up the hill.

After what was a tumultuous reception to *The Confessions of Nat Turner*, for which he was both criticized and celebrated for writing a novel from a black slave's point of view,

William began *Sophie's Choice*, arguably his masterwork. In it he tells the story of Sophie Zawistowski, a beautiful Polish survivor of Auschwitz, and Nathan Landau, a charismatic, violent-tempered young man obsessed with the Holocaust. Sophie's great secret, it turns out, is that at Auschwitz she was forced to choose which of her two young children, a son and daughter, was to live, and which was to die at the hands of the Nazis.

"Bill originally started with the scene in which Sophie has to choose. I remember saying, 'You can't do that because no mother will read further.' It was a gut reaction. Six years later, when Bill was done, the scene came at the end of the book."

Her advice was astute, for the suspense of the book hinges on the final revelation and its devastating outcome.

The conversation turns to the 1982 movie version of *Sophie's Choice*, directed by Alan J. Pakula, which featured Meryl Streep and Kevin Kline giving extraordinary performances as the doomed lovers.

"We knew Meryl before the movie was made, from the Yale Repertory Theatre. Alan told Bill he had chosen an Eastern European star—a very pretty, round blonde—and she was all set to go. We saw the audition tape, in fact. But Meryl came to Alan and begged to be auditioned. The rest is movie history."

The match of Streep and Kline proved electric. "Kevin had so much energy," Rose recalls. Then she mentions that there was once a four-hour version of the movie, which included "great scenes wherein Sophie and Nathan were roughest with each other." Regrettably, that long version appears to be lost, she says.

Rose's own life might have served as fodder for a novel, perhaps even an international thriller. In 1968, she traveled to the Soviet Union with her husband for an Afro-Asian writers' conference just as the Soviets were rolling tanks into Czechoslovakia. She and William met with authors, some in exile from a variety of repressive countries in the Middle and Far East. After Moscow, they walked around the streets and markets of

Tashkent, hearing incredible stories of suffering. "They were dissidents. Several of them gave me their manuscripts hoping I could help get them translated and published in the U.S.A. When I came home at the end of 1968, I went to Washington and tried to tell the State Department what was going on in gulags and beyond. The people I spoke to were not a bit interested."

A friend led her to Amnesty International. In early 1974, at Amnesty's behest, Rose traveled with her daughter Susanna to Santiago, Chile, just four months after General Augusto Pinochet had seized power in a bloody coup that reversed 40 years of democracy and caused the death of President Salvador Allende. Rose was charged with finding information on the whereabouts of Allende's ministers, suspected to be among "the disappeared"—those jailed and tortured by the Pinochet regime. "First Lady Hortense Allende was to speak at the U.N. in early February," wrote Rose in a Wellesley alumni publication, "and I had been chosen by Amnesty International to bring back detailed information on the atrocities to substantiate her report. And also to seek the whereabouts of artists and American students arrested and dragged into the infamous soccer stadium."

The assignment was plainly dangerous. "For company, and as a mother-daughter winter vacation 'cover,' I had brought my eldest child, Susanna, a savvy teenager who spoke excellent Spanish, which I certainly did not," recalled Rose in her account. "Had I properly understood Santiago's state of siege, or U.S. complicity, I would have come alone. Her skills saved me, more than once, from getting contacts or ourselves into major danger."

In Chile, Rose met with dissidents under secret circumstances, and collected important documents detailing the regime's abuses of human rights. As the days progressed, Pinochet's secret police became suspicious, even ransacking her hotel room, and finally Rose and her daughter fled aboard an airplane, with documents stashed in their clothes.

Sensing themselves followed even outside of the country (an obvious agent was placed in the seat next to them), they disembarked and hid in an airport restroom in Lima, Peru. They let their flight continue on without them, and then took an alternate route back to the U.S.

That year, Amnesty International issued prompt and detailed reports describing the Pinochet regime's horrific torture, kidnapping and execution of its own citizens; in the decade to come the organization would maintain political pressure on Chile and play an essential role in educating the international community on Pinochet's abuses.

In those years, Rose's commitment to the cause of human rights deepened into a lifelong mission. A founding member of Amnesty International USA, she still serves on its advisory board, as well as on those of Human Rights First, Human Rights Watch, and Equality Now. In addition to those roles, she has chaired PEN's Freedom to Write Committee and the Robert F. Kennedy Memorial Human Rights Award. But her interests clearly extend far beyond the political and into the realms of literature, science and the family. Currently she gives her energies to the boards of *The Paris Review*, the Brain & Creativity Institute at USC, the Academy of American Poets, and the Association to Benefit Children.

....

How much can a life hold? In the case of Rose Styron, it would appear the answer is, even more. A poet, she had published her work even before she was married. Her first book of poetry was *From Summer to Summer*, published in 1965, followed by *Modern Russian Poetry*, coedited with Olga Andreyev Carlisle in 1972, and *Thieves' Afternoon* in 1973. Her poems, as well as essays on human rights, book reviews and travel pieces, have appeared in a variety of anthologies and periodicals, including *The New York Review of Books*, *The Nation*, *Ms.*, and *The New Republic*. Most recently, she has published *By Vineyard Light*, a collection of poems centered on Martha's Vineyard, with photographs by Craig Dripps. Here, the poem "Katama":

This antique landscape rubbed by hand
shines through the mist like silvered hay.
Its hewn rail fence, greyed barn, sweet fields
where dusty birds hide, startled, focus day.

In the year after her husband died, she stayed in the house on Martha's Vineyard, looking out through a big window at the harbor while she wrote. "It is a pastoral setting framed by hedges," according to *The Martha's Vineyard Times*, "where the lawn rolls to the harbor and clusters of masts create changing canvasses of summer."

"The poems are so different from anything I've written before," she says. "A lot of them are about life with and without Bill. The poems were healing for me, a sort of diary of a year in grief. They've given me more distance. I'm going to go back and look at them, perhaps send a few out. Writing them kept me afloat." She pauses to consider, and adds, "What also really kept me afloat were my friends."

Back at Orso, dinner is done and dessert has disappeared. A car will soon be waiting outside. Daughters and granddaughters kiss Rose goodbye until next time and tomorrow she will fly to Martha's Vineyard to continue composing her poems and her unfinished, remarkable life — an optimist's life, let it be remembered. In the closing pages of *Sophie's Choice*, after Nathan and Sophie have died, Stingo, the narrator, understands that it isn't enough to merely endure life's trials. He must live with hope for the future, and here William Styron borrowed a phrase from the poet Emily Dickinson, "excellent and fair." One may perhaps be forgiven for borrowing this phrase again when pondering Rose Styron's optimism and her days ahead of family and work and service. Excellent and fair. ≈

OUT OF
THE SKY

....

by JERRY ADLER

illustrations by GALE ANTOKAL

HIS HANDS AND FACE WERE SINGED AS HE JUMPED FROM HIS
burning airplane, and in the air, the minus-50-degree cold stung his raw and blistered
skin. He fought the impulse to pull the rip cord on his parachute, remembering
what he'd been told in flight school: to fall as quickly as possible through the thin air
at 30,000 feet, before losing consciousness from lack of oxygen. So 2nd Lt. Samuel
Schimel fell toward a layer of broken clouds and the frozen ground of Germany below.
The date was November 2, 1944. He was on his 11th mission of the war, having just
qualified for a promotion to first lieutenant. The next day the order for his promotion
would arrive at his base in England, but he would not be there to receive it.

In a sunny apartment in Fort Lee, New Jersey, with views of Manhattan across the river, Sam Schimel opens a bulging scrapbook. The scars of his burns have faded over the years. At 87, his steps are slowed but firm, his voice still strong, his gaze steady beneath a modest thatch of white hair. It's not a huge stretch to imagine him as a young man in command of the mighty B-17, with 4,800 horsepower at his fingertips and the lives of nine crewmen in his hands.

In the crumbling pages of the scrapbook, you see him as he was then, his features strong, his hair dark and impressively thick. As the pages turn, snapshots of teenaged boys squinting into the sun give way to girls posing on the sand at the Jersey shore. Sam in his cadet uniform stands beside the Stearman biplane in which he learned to fly. Then suddenly there it is, a faded, creased telegram addressed to his father, David. "The Secretary of War," it reads, "desires me to express his deep regret that your son Second Lt. Samuel H. Schimel has been reported missing in action since Two November over Germany." That's all it says; tens of thousands just like it went out to parents all over the country.

Before he started flight training in 1943, Schimel had been in an airplane exactly once, in the 1920s: a barnstorming ride for five dollars from the future Newark Airport, then still a dirt airstrip. His military background was nonexistent. His grandfather started a wholesale butter-cheese-and-egg business in Jersey City in the early 1900s. His father worked as a salesman for a liquor wholesaler after his lunch wagon failed during the Great Depression. Schimel himself was studying to be an accountant, a profession that does not ordinarily overlap much with that of bomber pilot. He thought, like a lot of kids back then, that he should be fighting in the "good war." In no other capacity could a single individual do as much damage to the enemy as the pilot of a B-17, dropping tons of high explosives on the enemy's heartland.

"The way the military worked was like this: They gave you a list of specialties to choose from and you wrote down your top three choices in order, and then they sent you wherever you were needed, anyway. I chose first pilot on a bomber. I didn't want to fly fighters, because I didn't like flying around all by myself. I liked the idea of going up with a crew. I wanted to be in command. If I had gotten second [co]pilot, I would have been disappointed. So I got what I wanted, but I was probably just lucky.

"Believe it or not, at the time, there was no place I would rather be. I wasn't scared. You're in your early 20s, and you believe nothing can happen to you." As a Jew, and as an American, he welcomed the opportunity to destroy Germany's industrial capacity. "After the war, I met Jews who had been in the camps, and they told me how they cheered when they heard the bombers flying overhead, and that made me proud."

Almost every statistic about World War II is staggering, but one aspect of Schimel's experience captures the magnitude of the effort. It took an entire year, at camps and bases in a half-dozen states, to train a B-17 pilot, and many of them lasted only a few missions before they were shot down. Basic training was followed by officers' training, then flight school, then combat flight school, before you finally got to England and were assigned a plane and trained to fly in formation as low as 300 feet, below the clouds that often covered England and the Channel.

In the summer of 1944, Schimel found himself at an air base in East Anglia, in command of a B-17 in the mighty Eighth Air Force, which could put more than 1,000 bombers into the air at one time, in a stream of airplanes stretching 100 miles. Their job was precision bombing to destroy the infrastructure of the German war machine: factories, shipyards, railroads and refineries. Of course, that meant flying during the day, when it was easier for the Germans to see them. Schimel's crew was part of the squadron in the 457th Bombardment Group, nicknamed the Fireball Outfit.

A B-17 ordinarily carried a crew of 10, who trained together and stayed together until they completed their full tour of 25 missions, or were shot down. The expectation

"I remember calling up to Dick, my bombardier, and saying, 'Dick, there's a bomber stream way out there. What the hell are we doing here?'"

Almost immediately, they were under attack by German fighters....

was that they would live, die or be captured together, although sometimes a man would be killed aboard the plane, and the rest of his crew would make it back to base.

There's a picture of Schimel's crew, probably taken at combat flight school in Sioux City, Iowa. It shows the four officers, including Schimel, in their officers' hats, standing and grinning with their hands behind their back, behind the six enlisted men kneeling in their peaked garrison caps. In England, the crews were split up at first, so each man could fly with an experienced crew. In late September, Schimel took off on his first mission, to bomb the rail yards at Osnabrück. The rest of the crew—his second pilot, navigator, bombardier, radio operator, flight engineer and the four men who manned the machine guns—took places on other planes. The plane carrying Lt. Carl Ulander, the navigator, was shot down over Magdeburg, Germany. Suddenly, the war seemed a lot more serious to Schimel. In a second picture, taken in England shortly after, the grins are mostly gone on the members of his crew, now reduced to nine.

In an unfinished memoir he began a few years ago at the urging of a granddaughter, Sara Reichert, Schimel recalled Ulander, at a distance of more than 60 years, for his self-possession and the preternatural neatness of his uniform. On a particularly bumpy low-level training flight over the hills of South Dakota, Ulander got airsick but managed the feat of throwing up into the briefcase he always carried, leaving his uniform spotless. In reflecting on his war experience, Schimel combines a pilot's taciturnity with an accountant's precision, not a formula that lends itself to overt displays of sentiment. Many pilots named their planes, sometimes after sweethearts, or with a joke; Schimel never bothered. Asked how he felt about Ulander's death, he answers laconically, "Terrible." From then until the time he was shot down himself, he flew with a different navigator on every mission.

Flying combat over Germany was one of the most dangerous things you could do in the war. The bombers were attacked by antiaircraft artillery, or flak, and by fighter planes, faster and far more maneuverable than bombers. The B-17's principal adversary in the air was the Focke-Wulf 190, which carried four guns, including two that fired 20-millimeter shells, large enough to be called cannon. The fighters attacked in swarms, coming up behind the bombers, guns blazing, rolling away at the last instant. The B-17 wasn't defenseless, though. Twelve .50-caliber machine guns bristled from its fuselage for shooting back at the Germans, and it could take a surprising amount of damage and still fly, from which derived its nickname, the Flying Fortress. And by the time Schimel got into the war, the Americans had deployed their own long-range fighter, the P-51, which could escort the bombers all the way to their targets in Germany. Flying under the protection of their "little friends," the bomber crews felt much safer than their predecessors had a year earlier. But the P-51s couldn't guard against flak, and they could only protect bombers that stayed in formation. The Germans were still picking off strays whenever they found them.

Schimel never expected to take part in the November 2 mission, an attack by more than 1,000 aircraft on the huge refinery at Merseburg, near Leipzig. With gasoline scarce in the Reich, this was one of the most heavily defended targets in all of Germany. His crew was supposed to be off that day, having completed their 10th mission and earned a 48-hour pass to London, whose principal attraction was, he recalls, "girls who hadn't seen their men for three years." But because the Merseburg attack was an all-out effort, they were designated to fly as a "spare." The bombers flew in a formation designed for mutual protection, so if a plane dropped out, it was important to replace it. Schimel's orders were to trail his group and take the place of a plane if it turned back for any reason. "If by a designated longitude and latitude nobody aborted," Schimel wrote in his memoir, "we were to return to the field and take off for London." He followed the other planes halfway across the North Sea. His navigator told him they were 30 seconds' flying time from the turn-around point when another bomber dropped out of the formation with engine problems. Schimel pulled up to take its place.

There were clouds over Germany that day, and exactly what happened to the 48 planes of the 457th is uncertain. But it's known that they strayed off course, got separated from the main body of bombers, and dropped their bombs about 35 miles north of the intended target. That meant, of course, that when they turned for home, they were also 35 miles from the rest of the B-17s, and the P-51s that were escorting them. "I noticed the bomber stream was way off in the distance, miles away," Schimel wrote. "I remember calling up to Dick, my bombardier, and saying, 'Dick, there's the bomber stream way out there. What the hell are we doing here?'" Almost immediately they were under attack by German fighters, in closely spaced waves of 10 abreast, closing to within 100 yards of the blazing guns of the Fortresses. Schimel's plane was attacked from six o'clock, directly behind. Watching "our engine instruments collapsing before our eyes," frantically trying to keep aloft, Schimel and his copilot, Edward Grudzien, failed to notice that the bomb bay behind the cockpit—where the crew's oxygen tanks were stored—was on fire. Alerted by the flight engineer, Schimel hit a button to sound the alarm and struggled through the flames to a hatch in the belly of the plane, and stepped out into the sky.

"Those are my escape photos," Schimel says, pointing to a page in his scrapbook. "If we were shot down, and could make contact with the underground, they would try to get us out through Spain. They could forge papers but they were always short of film, so we carried these with us. I never got to use them."

Schimel landed in the middle of a town, and was immediately surrounded by German soldiers. He has no memory of the following hours, but his bombardier, Dick Coffman, who landed nearby, has told him that the Germans recognized that he was Jewish—his dog tag had a telltale "H," for "Hebrew"—and began beating him, lashing the blisters on his face and hands with their belt buckles. But the soldiers delivered him to a POW camp. Airmen weren't always so lucky; if civilians got to them first, they were sometimes beaten to death.

Apart from Coffman, he didn't know the fate of the rest of his crew. They were nine altogether; to save weight for the long flight, one of the two waist gunners, an affable Italian-American named Tony DeMaro, had been left behind on that mission. Some days later, Schimel was brought in for questioning by a suave German officer. He gave his name, rank and serial number, as required by the Geneva Convention, and declined to answer any more questions. "It doesn't matter," the officer said nonchalantly. "We know you're from the 457th. We have the rest of your crew, the ones who are still alive." It was from this officer that Schimel learned that the three men from the back of the plane — the tail gunner, the waist gunner and the ball turret gunner in a transparent cage suspended from the belly of the plane — never made it out. "There was nothing I could have done about it," Schimel says now. "But I felt terrible about it. I was in command of the plane. The men were my responsibility."

In the scrapbook, another telegram to his father is dated December 9: "Report just received through the International Red Cross states that your son, Second Lieutenant Samuel H. Schimel, is a prisoner of war of the German government." On another page is Schimel's POW file from the German camp, which in neat handwriting, under "Religion" (the word is the same in German), reads "Mosaisch." And wrapped in plastic is a small piece of ersatz bread he saved from one of his meals while in captivity. That it has survived all this time is testimony to its composition, which Schimel assumes was mostly sawdust.

He was moved from camp to camp, usually in boxcars — where, ironically, he nervously waited out a bombing raid on a rail yard, grateful for once that the air force missed its target. There was one move that took place on foot through the snow, pulling his belongings on a sled made of bed slats. He was often hungry, losing 25 pounds or so over six months, but his health didn't suffer too badly. By late 1944, the Germans knew they were losing, and they had no incentive to mistreat prisoners — especially ones from America, the country they were counting on to save them from the much worse fate of being overrun by the Red Army. Did he experience anti-Semitism as

a prisoner? Yes, Schimel says, from some of the English officers held in the same camps. One German officer interrogated him intensively about his religion—but, to be fair, he was also interrogated intensively by a group of American officers, a precaution to root out German plants or spies. "They asked me questions about baseball, which actually I didn't know anything about," he says. "But I guess they recognized my Jersey City accent."

His last camp was Stalag 7A, outside Munich, where he arrived in early February 1945. Hungry and cold, he waited out the last few months of the war, listening for the sound of artillery in the distance. Around noon one day at the end of April, tanks began to appear around the camp, and he looked up and saw an American flag flying from the church steeple in the town nearby. Right on the heels of the GIs were women from the Red Cross, bearing something he thought he might never see again: doughnuts.

A final telegram to Schimel's father, June 15, 1945: "The Chief of Staff of the Army directs me to inform you your son 2/Lt Schimel Samuel H is being returned to the United States within the near future and will be given an opportunity to communicate with you upon arrival."

First, though, he had to see Paris. From a camp in Le Havre, where they were awaiting a ship back to the States, Schimel and a buddy wrangled a pass and drew some of the thousands in back pay they were owed. They stretched $300 and a three-day pass to a week and a half, much of which was spent in an apartment shared by several young French nurses. Finally Schimel turned to his friend and said, "We'd better get back to Le Havre, because if we don't leave now we'll never go back home."

They sailed for America in June, and arrived in Virginia a week later, to a band on the wharf playing "Don't Fence Me In." They traveled by train to Fort Dix, New Jersey, a 90-minute drive from his home in Atlantic City.

"We'll be right down to pick you up," his father said. "Don't bother," Schimel replied. He had gone away as a youngster, and returned as a man, someone who had flown an airplane and commanded men in war, fought battles five miles in the air and survived forced marches through enemy territory. He was happy to see his family again, but he wanted to savor another few hours of irresponsible freedom first. "I'll hitchhike," he said. And he did.

The final section of the scrapbook, and the ones he kept for decades to come, documents a very different life: photos of his first wife Bernice Miller, who died of cancer more than 40 years ago, and his wife now, Marylou Lionells. There are pages and pages of their lives together, their daughters, Marjorie and Dale, their travels around the world, the boats they owned, the fish they caught. Friends, grandchildren, great-grandchildren. The rewards of owning a successful accounting practice. But his most precious possession, his pilot's wings, are framed and mounted behind glass, along with his Purple Heart, his World War II combat medal, the Air Medal (an eagle with two lightning bolts in his claws) and a Prisoner of War Medal (an eagle surrounded by barbed wire). It's been a good life, all in all, and, apart from the loss of Bernice, a lucky one. Being shot down over Germany was scary, but once he landed, at least there was no one shooting at him anymore.

There's no way of knowing how things might have turned out if the 457th hadn't gone off course en route to Merseburg. Probably Schimel would have made it back to England, to fly another day. He had 14 missions left to fly on his tour, and although they were gradually becoming less risky, there was still plenty of fight left in the Luftwaffe. On March 24, 1945, with less than two months left in the war, the 457th took part in a raid against a German airfield at Hopsten. One of the planes in Schimel's squadron lost part of one wing when an antiaircraft shell exploded nearby; it went into a spin and crashed on the ground, killing six of the nine airmen aboard.

One of the casualties was Tony DeMaro, the waist gunner from Schimel's crew, the only one who didn't take part in the attack on Merseburg. Ten men started the war together, flying in Schimel's airplane. Counting Ulander, the navigator, DeMaro and the three who died over Merseburg, half were still alive by the time it was over. Schimel was one of them.

He was, as he says, lucky. ≈

Called to Serve

by JENNIFER BARRETT

illustrations by LAUREN SIMKIN BERKE

ONE AFTERNOON IN THE SPRING OF 1943, MARY LOUISE CHAPMAN—Mary Lou, to most who know her—was flipping through an issue of *Mademoiselle* when a small photograph caught her eye: a U.S. soldier and a pretty young woman in a Red Cross uniform, curls peeking out from below her blue cap, were sitting side by side on a grassy knoll in the English countryside. *Now* that *is for me*, she thought to herself.

The country was at war. Newsreels were full of reports of Allied bombing campaigns in Europe and bloody battles in North Africa. Gas and coffee rationing were in effect. Soldiers were beginning to trickle back home, some in flag-draped coffins. A growing number of porches were covered in black bunting.

But Chapman was working as a physical education teacher at a school in a leafy, upscale suburb of New York, feeling about as far removed from the action as the restless 24-year-old could stand to be. The image in the magazine looked exotic (at that point, she'd never traveled outside the country — she'd hardly left the state — except for a handful of car trips across the border to Canada). Yet the Red Cross uniform was reassuringly familiar.

Her mother served as chairwoman of the Red Cross chapter in Oriskany, the small town in upstate New York (population: 1,200) where Chapman had grown up with one brother and three step-siblings. Before she was old enough to start school, she was helping organize packets for door-to-door fund drives, counting Red Cross membership pins and folding pamphlets. "My mother was a big influence. She never turned down anybody who came to our house seeking help," says Chapman. "Service was important to her."

As a young woman, Chapman found it was becoming increasingly important to her as well. She volunteered for an overnight shift at a switchboard, taking calls from civilian plane spotters like her mother, who watched the skies at night for suspicious aircraft. But this opportunity seemed more exciting than manning the phones. The photo made the Red Cross worker's life overseas seem romantic. By the end of the semester, Chapman had signed up and was preparing to ship out.

"What's so hard to explain to people who didn't live through World War II is that *everybody* was doing something to help the war effort then," says Chapman. "I wanted to do something meaningful."

Weeks later, the petite, blue-eyed brunette found herself peering up a ramp on the RMS *Aquitania*, as sirens blared, worriedly scanning the dark skies above for enemy aircraft. The British ocean liner, which had been drafted into service for the war, was strafed twice by low-flying German pilots during its transatlantic voyage. Though none of the bullets hit the ship, its passengers — hundreds of uniformed soldiers and Red Cross support staff like Chapman — were not allowed to go above deck for the entire trip. This wasn't exactly what Chapman had envisioned as she'd gazed at the dreamy image in the magazine.

Still, she'd longed for adventures that would take her far beyond the cloistered walls of her suburban school. And she got them. Once the *Aquitania* docked in England, Chapman and three other Red Cross workers were assigned to a "clubmobile," a British bus retrofitted to accommodate a kitchen with a doughnut-making machine, a stove and a 50-cup coffee urn; a large flap that could be opened to serve soldiers; and a lounge with built-in benches. Over the next several months, the four were dispatched to B-24 bases throughout England and Scotland to provide troops with doughnuts and coffee. They'd work all day, then spend the night at the nearby homes of families who'd offered to host the women.

The soldiers were so delighted to see a female face and to eat something besides rations that they'd often mob the clubmobile when it arrived at a base, and many would hang around long after they'd finished their treats. Chapman and her crew could serve 200 troops or more in a day, but she still remembers some of them vividly. One was a gunner to whom she agreed to lend her dog tags for good luck before he left on a bomber mission over Germany. It would be more than a year before she saw him again, emerging with other emaciated prisoners from a newly liberated camp in Germany, where her clubmobile was dispatched the day after the war ended in Europe. His B-24 had been shot down—but he'd miraculously survived, though her dog tags had not. "They're at the bottom of the North Sea," he informed her.

Though Chapman was far from the battlefronts when she served in England, there were constant reminders of the war. The windows of her host family's home were covered with blackout curtains. When she traveled to London during time off, she'd often be awakened in the night by the loud rasping sound of 25-foot-long, self-propelled "buzz bombs" that rained down on the city, sending those below scurrying for cover before the ordnance exploded. During one visit, a hotel staff member woke her up and sent her to the basement to huddle with other guests as bombs exploded nearby. In the underground subway stations, families stretched out on bunk beds that had been hastily assembled. They were either too frightened to sleep in their homes, or they'd lost them. Chapman often spotted new piles of debris where buildings had stood for hundreds of years. "Sure, you are a little scared," she says, "but you don't ever think you're going to get it."

Except once. After D-day (June 6, 1944), when nearly 150,000 U.S. troops stormed the beaches of Normandy, Chapman and her crew were sent to catch up with the XX Army Corps, which was zigzagging across the countryside south of Paris. She spent weeks following in a clubmobile, as they pushed east through Germany toward Austria. When they stopped overnight, the Red Cross workers would often stay in abandoned homes. Once, when she entered the basement of a house she'd been assigned, she came face to face with a German soldier in full uniform. "That was one time I remember being really frightened," she says. Fortunately, he turned and fled, and so did she.

There were happier memories: the flowers that grateful French townspeople showered on them as their convoy passed through, for example, and the bottles of bubbly she shared with soldiers when they were stationed in the Champagne region. "But if I got a shower once a week, I was lucky," she says. And the rations they ate from unmarked green tins were so tasteless that when some navy pilots gave them white bread, she says, "We ate it like cake."

The toughest assignment she got was on a train carrying wounded soldiers. Chapman still remembers feeding tiny pieces of a doughnut to a soldier burned so badly his entire head was hidden under gauze wrap, except for a tiny hole over his mouth. "That's the only time I ever cried," she says.

Chapman returned to New York in September 1945 a changed woman. She'd lost her Red Cross field job the day after the war ended, but she knew she'd found her calling. She turned down a teaching job and made her way to the national Red Cross headquarters in Washington, D.C., where she got a temporary position helping soldiers fill out medical paperwork. Then a fellow clubmobile worker who'd become a close friend phoned from California to see if Chapman wanted to take a full-time job with her at the Red Cross chapter in Long Beach. Chapman jumped at the chance.

About three years later, she moved north to the Bay Area chapter, where she became the director of youth services and, later, assistant manager. Chapman would remain a full-time staff member there for nearly 35 years. She would have stayed even longer had she not hit the mandatory retirement age of 65 in 1984. Even after giving up her full-time position, she's continued to help out with specific projects. "She's devoted her life to the organization," says Loulie Sutro, who worked for Chapman at the Red Cross for about four years in the 1960s and has since become a close friend. "She is a true altruist, and she believes in the tenets of the Red Cross."

Chapman had married a successful physician, Max, whom she'd met in 1953 when he was Pacific Area director of the Red Cross Blood Services Program. "So I'm sure she didn't have to work," says Sutro. In fact, most of their friends had stopped working when they got married. But Chapman says simply, "I stayed at the Red Cross because I loved it."

More than anything, though, Chapman was devoted to her family. Though she and Max never had children of their own, she continues to have a close bond with Max's children from a prior marriage, Betty and John. "My stepchildren, along with their spouses and children—they are my family," she says. "I've always loved young people."

In her work at the Red Cross, Chapman has helped young people get involved in their communities and the world—one of the personal achievements of which she is most proud. And many of those who went through her youth leadership programs still recall her fondly, decades later. "I remember Mary Lou as having a wicked sense of humor. She was tough but incredibly compassionate," says Rep. Jackie Speier, a congresswoman from California who credits the Red Cross program, and Chapman, "for setting me on the course for public service."

Chapman continued to work at the Red Cross after her husband suffered a massive stroke that left him paralyzed on the right side, about 15 years after they were married.

But almost all her free time was dedicated to his recovery. For months, he couldn't talk, walk or write. But slowly, with the help of Chapman and therapists, he was able to speak again, to walk with a brace and to write with his left hand. She made sure they still traveled and held on to their season tickets to the San Francisco Symphony. Years later, after he broke his hip in a fall, she had a special trolley car constructed to take him up the two flights of wooden stairs to the front door of their hillside Berkeley home. ("Max loved this house," she says simply. "He wouldn't think of moving.")

"I was always impressed by the way that this wonderful lady was able to keep him alive and happy and to allow him to live as normal a life as he could," says Michael Jang, a sociologist in San Francisco who participated in one of the youth leadership programs Chapman ran in 1959 and who returned later as a Red Cross volunteer. "She took care of him, and never complained, and did everything she could to help him live an independent life after the stroke — and he did, for a long time."

Max died in 1990, more than 20 years after he'd suffered the stroke. "I think the whole experience made better people of both of us," says Chapman, dabbing at her eyes with a tissue as she talks about her late husband. A large framed photo of him still sits on the television console in the living room of the home they shared, beside a large globe and shelves crammed with gourmet cookbooks like *The Six-Minute Soufflé* and *The Art of Baking*.

These days, Chapman's cooking is squeezed in among a growing list of activities. She is a voracious reader on a variety of subjects — in early July, she was reading *Watching Baseball Smarter* (her husband had been a huge baseball fan) — and tries to give away close to 100 books each year to make room for new ones. She plays tennis three times a week with partners who are 20 years younger, or more. ("Let's just say I'd rather have her as my doubles partner than my opponent," says Rev. Bruce O'Neill, the 42-year-old rector of the St. Clement's Episcopal Church she attends.) On Thursday mornings, she drives to San Francisco for the weekly hair appointment she's kept for decades, despite the sometimes hour-long drive. She wears her sandy-colored hair short and stylishly flipped out, above her red-framed glasses and lipstick. She plays competitive bridge at least one night a week and often has dinner out with friends; and she still has season tickets to the San Francisco Symphony and the ballet.

When Chapman left her full-time Red Cross job in 1984, a group of donors raised enough money to create a fund in her name and that of her assistant, which she continues to help oversee. Each year, the Chapman-Holcombe Fund pays for a few international high school students to travel to the Bay Area for three weeks to volunteer with the American Red Cross and receive leadership training. Two teens from Gambia, for example, learned how U.S. nonprofit groups were dealing with the AIDS crisis in San Francisco so they could apply the knowledge to their small West African country, where approximately 20,000 suffer from HIV/AIDS. Teenagers from more than 30 countries have participated in the program so far. "The fact that she has stayed connected has helped the program live on," says Kristin Tewksbury, a senior manager of youth services for the Bay Area chapter. "We're the only Red Cross chapter in the country with a program and fund like this, and it's really due to Mary Lou and her interest in international service."

No matter how busy Chapman's social calendar gets, there will always be time for the Red Cross and for volunteering. On Wednesdays, she now volunteers at the front desk of the Alta Bates Summit Medical Center, where her husband was treated. ("I just thought they were so good to Max," she says, by way of explanation.) And she is now completing an unpaid two-year term as director of the altar guild at her Episcopal church, where she helps prepare for weekly services. In July, she was also busy preparing recipes for homemade bread and a "dazzling rice and peas dish" for this year's Red Cross interns, who'd be flying in from Barbados and Suriname two days after she returned from a 10-day vacation in Hawaii.

"I just can't imagine not volunteering, ever," says Chapman, who will be 90 in February 2009. "I guess it's a sense of purpose. You have something that you're responsible for, and you feel that sense of responsibility to keep it going."

And that, she says, has helped keep her going as well. ⪦

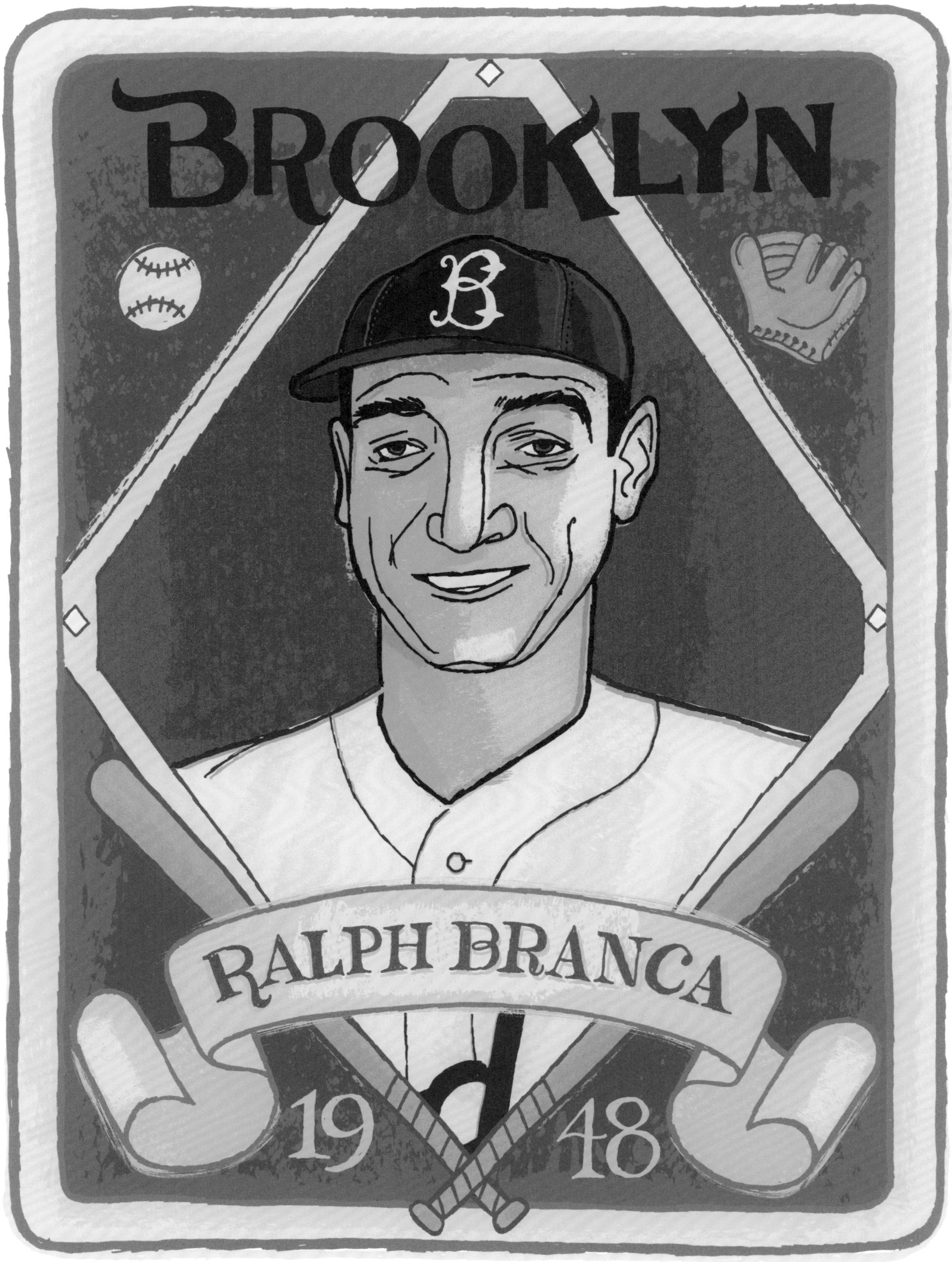

BROOKLYN
RALPH BRANCA
19
48

High Heat

by IRA BERKOW

illustrations by PAUL ROGERS

IT HAPPENS LESS FREQUENTLY THESE DAYS, BUT MORE THAN 57 YEARS later, 57 years after that moment that will not die, it is mentioned to Ralph Branca, or he is prepared for it to be mentioned.

Branca, his hair gray but looking fit and younger than his 82 years, sat in a canopied outdoor restaurant near his home in a suburb of New York City, where he lives with his wife, Ann, the woman he married just 17 days after it happened, those 57-plus years ago. Over lunch of iced tea and a chicken Caesar salad ("no croutons, please"), he now recalled his days as a major-league pitcher, the drama and the joys, and the uncommon life he led after that long-ago moment.

"Ralph is a very intelligent man who has an understanding of the world and his place in it," Bobby Valentine, the one-time manager of the Texas Rangers and New York Mets, and the son-in-law of Branca, said in a recent e-mail. Valentine, who married Branca's daughter Mary, is now the manager with the Chiba Lotte Marines of Japan's

Pacific League. He said his father-in-law "has always been understanding of my situation, whatever it was, and when things were bad, Ralph has always been there."

It is hardly surprising that he would be understanding. At first, in the moments and hours and days—maybe even years—after it happened, in the haze of a late afternoon, at 3:58 p.m., on October 3, 1951, in the Polo Grounds in upper Manhattan, he was burdened with it. How do you deal with personal disaster, even if it comes in the form of a game that little boys can play?

As time went on, however, he slowly came out of, as he called it, "shock." At some point he began to talk openly about it—and even joke about it. He would be invited to speak to various groups, whether it was about baseball or at investment conferences or in college classrooms, and he had a running gag:

"After two questions from the audience, I'd say, 'Isn't somebody going to ask me how I felt?' It was always the third question."

Looking back, it all seems so mundane, if not silly, that people should invest so much of their hearts and emotion in a game, even that particular game.

Essentially, a pitcher, Ralph Branca of the Brooklyn Dodgers, comes in to pitch relief in the bottom of the ninth inning in that quirky, horseshoe-shaped ballpark on Coogan's Bluff. His team was ahead 4–2, there were two men on base and one out. He delivers a pitch, a pitch "at the chin," which would have been called a ball had the batter, Bobby Thomson of the New York Giants, let it sail by, but Thomson takes an uppercut swing and lofts a fly ball. Branca watches, pleading silently, *Sink, sink!*

But let's step back to give a sweep of the situation: This was the third and final play-off game, the tiebreaker, for the National League pennant. (The Giants had won the first game, the Dodgers the second.) If Branca gets two outs, the Dodgers head for Yankee Stadium to play in the World Series the following day.

Branca entered the game to pitch to Thomson after his manager, Charlie Dressen, phoned from the dugout to the bullpen to have him relieve the starting pitcher, Don Newcombe. Branca had been throwing well in the warmups and felt strong.

"I felt confident," Branca recalled. "Even with the pennant on the line, I didn't feel pressure."

A 6-foot-3, 220-pound, hard-throwing right-hander, Ralph, then 25—with "golden muscles in his pitching arm," as the former Dodger president Branch Rickey had once described him—whizzed his first pitch down the middle to Thomson. He let it go for strike one. "It was about a 93–94-mile-an-hour fastball," recalled Branca.

The Dodgers fans in the crowd of 34,320 howled with anticipation at the called strike. It silenced the Giants fans, who had been on their feet as their team rallied to score one run in this ninth inning and now, after one out, had managed to put those runners on second and third.

It may be difficult for current fans to truly contemplate the intense rivalry between these two teams, from adjoining boroughs of New York City. After all, both the Giants and the Dodgers departed by the end of the decade for California. Their ballparks, the Polo Grounds and Ebbets Field, were reduced to rubble by the wrecking ball, apartment buildings constructed in their place. But if, in that era of flannel uniforms and players quaintly leaving their gloves on the field when they came in to bat, it wasn't a matter of life and death for fans of the winners and losers, it was surely the sporting equivalent.

Years later, Newcombe himself recalled the rivalry: "Just the names of the players in those days could get you juiced up—we had Jackie and Campy and Furillo and Erskine and Duke and Reese, they had Dark and Willie and Maglie and Jansen and Monte Irvin."

And to add unnecessary spice to the mix, the Giants manager was the combative former Dodgers manager, Leo ("The Lip") Durocher.

With the current glut of sports and teams, it may be difficult to contemplate how important baseball was in the American culture. "There were only 16 teams in major-league baseball at the time, where there are 30 now," recalled Branca. "And the only postseason was the World Series. A play-off occurred only when two teams were tied for first place at the end of the season, and our play-off was only the second in National League history. Now there are play-offs after play-offs. The NBA, the NFL, the big tennis and golf tournaments, auto racing—none of it had the hold on fans that baseball did. From a standpoint of general interest, the other sports were in their infancy. Television was in its infancy. Baseball was king. Baseball in New York took on a kind of cult obsession. And in Brooklyn especially, the fans had a passionate love affair with our team."

Add this to the fact that the Giants had made a fantastic comeback at season's end. They had trailed the seemingly uncatchable Dodgers by 13½ games by August 11.

ONE OUT, LAST of the Ninth . . .

Ralph Branca PITCHES,

Thomson takes a strike

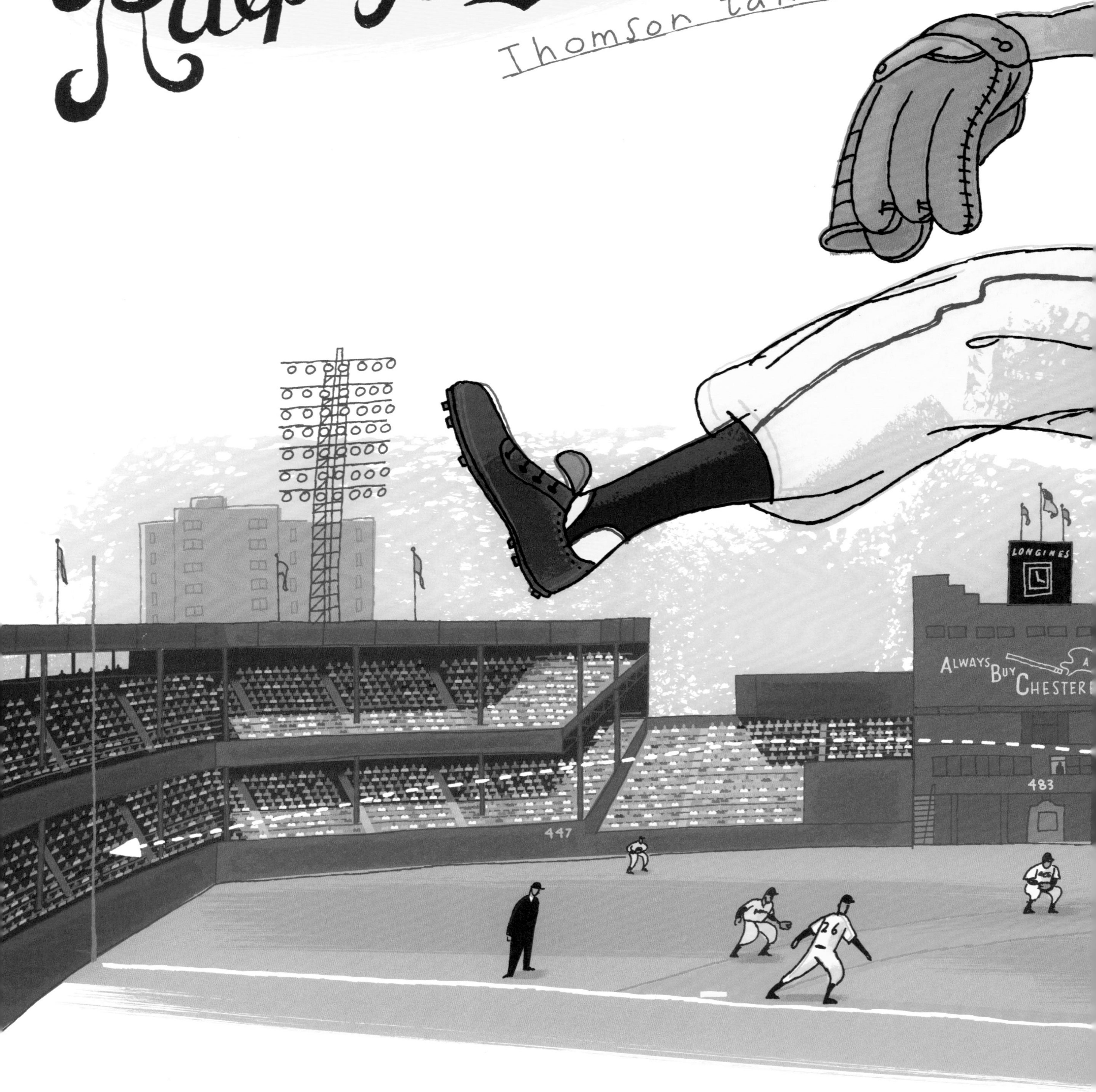

But the Giants won a blistering 37 of their remaining 44 games while the Dodgers stumbled and squandered their lead, putting their fans in a panic. To even create a play-off situation and tie the Giants for first place on the last day of the season, the Dodgers had to beat the Phillies—in 14 innings yet—on a home run by Jackie Robinson.

Branca, in 1951, was still one of the most formidable pitchers in baseball. In his first full season in the big leagues, in 1946, he was, at age 20, the starting pitcher in the first play-off game in N.L. history, but lost to the Cardinals. The next season, he won 21 games, tied for second in the league. He made the all-star team that year—and the following two seasons as well. He suffered a shoulder ailment in 1950—had a 7–9 record—but had recovered by the following fateful season to post a 13–12 record and a strong 3.26 earned run average. He was fourth in the league in allowing fewest hits per inning, and fourth in the league in strikeouts per game, with just over five. He started the first game of the '51 play-offs and pitched a solid eight innings, giving up three runs on just five hits, but one of those hits was a home run to—who else?—Bobby Thomson, with a man on. The Dodgers lost 3–1.

Now Branca hoped to settle matters by striking out Thomson. From the mound, he looked down to Rube Walker, a broad, squatting target behind the plate, for the sign for his second pitch. One finger: fastball. Yes, he'd throw it high and inside for a ball, setting up Thomson for a curveball strike on the outside corner.

Alas, it wasn't to be.

Branca gripped the ball with a hand so large he could nearly touch thumb and middle finger around the sphere. He wound up and threw, his body so low while unleashing his pitch that his right knee, as usual, scraped the ground. Lean Bobby Thomson swung and the batted ball flew skyward and began to dip and dip, but fell just beyond the hopeless reach of the left fielder, Andy Pafko, who slumped against the wall in frustration. The ball landed in the first row of the stands, as fans scrambled for it.

"The Giants win the pennant! The Giants win the pennant!" screamed Russ Hodges, the Giants' radio announcer, into his microphone in the broadcast booth, as three Giants runners jubilantly circled the bases.

An 18-year-old Dodger fan living on East 17th Street in the Flatbush section of Brooklyn named Maury Allen, who was to become a distinguished New York sportswriter, had cut class and gone to a high school friend's home down the street from where he lived with his parents to watch the game.

"My friend was one of the few who had a TV set in those days," recalled Allen. "As soon as Thomson hit the home run I bolted out of his house, slamming the door, and ran to my apartment, slammed the front door, slammed my bedroom door and fell sobbing onto my bed. I wouldn't come out of my room. My mother called me for dinner, but I refused to move from my pillow. I didn't come out of my room until the next morning. A lot of us Dodgers fans felt it was the end of the world."

As Branca turned from the mound and started toward the center-field clubhouse, the number on his uniform, as the great sports columnist Red Smith wrote, "looked huge. Thirteen."

Some few minutes later, after this most wrenching 5–4 loss, a photographer took a now famous shot of Branca slumped on the clubhouse steps, capless, his head buried in his hands in complete despair.

Later, after he had showered, Ralph went to the stadium parking lot, where he was met by his fiancée Ann and her cousin, the priest Pat Rowley. "I remember saying to him, 'Father, why me?'" said Branca. "And he said, 'Because God knew your faith would be strong enough to bear the cross.'"

Has it? Branca was asked. He nodded. "I think so, yes," he replied.

It has been some cross to bear.

The moment has been called "The Miracle at Coogan's Bluff." The home run has gone into legend as "The Shot Heard 'Round the World." In 1999, the U.S. Postal Service issued a stamp of the home run, which, along with 14 other subjects, was to represent the 1950s in its Celebrate the Century program (along with, to name two, *Drive-In Movies* and *I Love Lucy*). The term "walk-off home run" had not yet been invented. But that's what it was, the game ended, the pennant decided, on that one pitch, that one swing. Nothing quite like it has ever again taken place in baseball.

Forty years after the home run, in the May 27, 1991, issue of *The New Yorker*, Roger Angell, the superb baseball writer for that magazine, noted that Thomson's home run "stands as the most vivid single moment, the grand exclamation point, in the history of the pastime." Nothing, it seems, has happened to change that observation.

After his long-planned wedding in mid-October 1951, Branca, like most players, had to work during the off-season to supplement his baseball income—he sold insurance. The highest salary he earned in baseball was $17,500, in the 1949 season, about $5,000 above the average for players that year. (Branca, in off-seasons, also completed two years at New York University.)

Fred Wilpon remembers Branca well. "He was a kind of idol of mine," said Wilpon, chairman of the board and CEO of the New York Mets. Wilpon had been a rising pitching star and Brooklyn Lafayette high-school teammate of Sandy Koufax in the early 1950s. He said Branca "was used as an example by my parents. Ralph had gone to New York University, and my parents said, 'See, there's a fine, intelligent young man who went to college before he entered baseball.' I had wanted to follow in that path." (Wilpon suffered an arm injury, ending his baseball career, but did graduate from the University of Michigan.)

In 1952, Branca injured his back in spring training and struggled on the mound. "Some people wrote that I had trouble pitching because it was psychological, that I was suffering from the aftereffects of the home run," he said. "But it wasn't. It was the soreness in my back. Maybe, though, I was trying too hard to come back, pressing too hard to make good."

He pitched in only 16 games in 1952—he had appeared in 42 the season before—and finished with a 4-2 record. He was traded to Detroit the next season—the back hindering his pitching motion—to the Yankees the following year, was in the minor leagues in 1955, came back to Brooklyn in 1956, pitching in one game with two shutout innings, and then was released, his baseball career over. He was 30 years old. He had spent part or all of 12 seasons in the big leagues (he first appeared briefly for the Dodgers in 1944, when he was 18), finishing with a fine 88–68 won–lost record and a lifetime earned run average of 3.79.

But it was with the Tigers, in 1954, that Branca was told something that stunned him, and years later would stun followers of baseball. "Thomson knew what I was going to throw him," said Branca, the smile on his face disappearing. "Ted Gray, a pitcher on the Tigers and a friend of mine, said to me one day, 'Ralph, I don't know if I should tell you, but—'

"He told me that a former player on the Giants, then with the St. Louis Browns, a reserve outfielder named Earl Rapp, had told him of the Giants' elaborate scheme for stealing the signs." Herman Franks, a coach with the Giants, peered through a Wollensak telescope while seated in the shadow of Leo Durocher's office in center field. He would then tell Hank Schenz, a utility infielder sitting alongside Franks, what the pitch was and Schenz would hit a button to relay the information through a cleverly wired buzzer system to both the Giants' bullpen and dugout.

The bullpen was located in deep right-center field, barely to the right of the mound — an easy target for the hitter to observe. One inning the bullpen gave the signs using Sal Yvars, a reserve catcher, who used a baseball or a towel as his signaling device. The next inning the dugout would shout out special words, such as "Sock it" for a fastball, "Be ready" for a curve and "Watch it" as the third pitch, either a slider or changeup.

"Stealing signs is not all that unusual in baseball — if it's on the field, that's part of the game. But the way the Giants did it, going off the field, into the sanctity of the clubhouse, and using a buzzer system to relay signs, well...." Branca paused, without a smile. "They made heroes out of those guys. I thought — I think — going that far to tell hitters what was coming was one of the most despicable acts in baseball."

In his book, *The Echoing Green: The Untold Story of Bobby Thomson, Ralph Branca and the Shot Heard Round the World*, published in 2006, author Joshua Prager detailed the revelation. He quotes Giants catcher Sal Yvars telling him that he relayed the sign of the pitch to Thomson. Thomson, however, said he had no foreknowledge of the pitch he belted for the historic home run.

"Thomson denied it to me," said Branca. "I like Bobby, but I was disappointed that he wouldn't admit that he knew what was coming."

For his part, Thomson said, "I wasn't nervous when I came to bat, I was numb."

Thomson later told Branca: "I was just thinking as I walked to the plate, 'Give yourself a chance — watch and wait, watch and wait. Don't be too anxious.'"

Years later, Thomson told this reporter: "I try to downplay the home run. I'm grateful people remember, but life goes on." Could Thomson possibly empathize with Branca? "I guess you can get a little tired of hearing about that homer.

"And I know it's been kind of a burden to Ralph. He once said, 'Why me?' But I remember the next day, when we were playing the Yankees in the World Series, he took a picture with me and he was joking and choking me. I thought it took a lot for him to do that, and said a lot about Ralph Branca the person."

"I remember saying to him, 'Father, why me?'

And he said, 'Because God knew your faith would be strong enough to bear the cross.'"

Branca added that he and Thomson have done some card-signing shows together: "We got to know each other and became friends."

Branca said, "People talk about the homer less and less. Young people aren't so tied to it. To them it's ancient history, like the Civil War."

Some of the responses he's heard over the years about the home run have made him laugh. "One guy said, 'I was in Ebbets Field and saw Thomson hit the homer.' I said, 'You must have great eyes to see through the buildings all the way to the Polo Grounds.'"

When Branca left baseball, he went into the life-insurance business full-time. "And I made a success of it," he said. "You work on commission in this business, and you have your ups and downs, but overall I was fairly consistent.

"Strange thing is that my 'notoriety,' or being so-called infamous, for throwing that pitch, helped my business. I was never shy about being in public. I've been out of baseball for more than 50 years, and people still recognize me on the street. I know who I am. And if a client is curious about it, I'd talk with him about it. Most people are well-meaning. But there are some who like to zing people. You'd hear stage whispers—'Bobby Thomson.' Yeah, but how many guys play big-league baseball? How many guys have dreamed of it? I did it."

He and Ann, a graduate of Marymount College, also brought up two daughters who had professional careers: Mary became a dental hygienist and Patti became a special education teacher in the Westchester school district.

Branca developed into a superb golfer (handicap went as low as four but is higher today) and still enjoys playing in charity events. He has always had an exceptional singing voice. A baritone, he has sung the national anthem at ballparks, Hall of Fame induction ceremonies and baseball banquets. "I still put on the radio when I'm driving and sing along with the songs," he said. "I did it as a player," driving the 40 minutes from his home in Mt. Vernon, N.Y., to Ebbets Field. "I've always found singing uplifting."

For 16 years, until 2003, Branca was the first CEO and chairman of BAT, the Baseball Assistance Team, which has provided financial help for more than 1,500 needy or indigent ex-major-league players, umpires and their families. (Branca was also one of the organization's cofounders, along with several that included Joe Garagiola and Warren Spahn.)

"For example, we got a prosthetic for my old teammate Sandy Amoros, when he had a leg amputated," said Branca. "He had been living above a garage in Miami, and we got him an apartment. For him and many other players and families that were having hard times, we've paid rent and put food on the table, and got clothes for them. We got requests, looked into them, and then saw if there was something we could do to help."

Branca also cited a former Dodgers World Series pitcher, Nick Willhite, who became homeless and an alcoholic. He was on the verge of suicide. He called an old teammate, Stan Williams, to say good-bye. Williams wisely suggested contacting BAT. Willhite did, and was rescued. He recovered in a rehab center to the extent that he was reunited with his family and took a job with the Utah Alcoholism Foundation in Salt Lake City.

Who are the players who need help? Some didn't make a lot of money in baseball, or squandered it on bad investments. Some, like Amoros, had few skills developed other than playing baseball, and some, like Willhite, had some business setbacks, got depressed, and suffered a downhill spiral. Branca and his hand-picked committee of New York executives held annual BAT dinners in Manhattan that raised millions of dollars for the organization.

Branca now is an active board member of Sports Angels, a not-for-profit group that provides assistance to other organizations that serve disabled and disadvantaged children, from the mentally and physically handicapped to victims of Hurricane Katrina.

When asked how he would like to be remembered, Branca replied. "I don't know … I guess first my work with BAT. And then, well, I was a good young pitcher. I started the first two play-off games, in 1946 and 1951. I was the starting pitcher in the opening game of the 1947 World Series. I made three All-Star teams, and was the starting pitcher in one of them. From 1947 through 1949, I won 48 games and lost 26. People forget how good I was."

He sat back in his chair on the veranda, still thinking about how he'd like to be remembered. "And," he said at last, "as the guy who threw the home-run pitch." He smiles at his ironic joke.

His daughters Patti and Mary see it differently, knowing the insults he endured from abusive fans. "We think Dad should be remembered as the quiet hero who remained silent while being crucified."

From across the table, Ralph Branca appeared to be a man who, for over half a century, has indeed been strong enough to bear his singular cross. ≈

MONSTER LOVE

....

by PETER HERBST

illustrations by JOSH COCHRAN

THE DARK LORDS MUST BE SMILING. I'M AT THE MIDTOWN MANHATTAN office of Richard Gordon, the horror-movie producer who managed to bring both Bela Lugosi and Boris Karloff back to life during a long and fruitful career, and it's actually Friday the 13th! Not that Gordon, a small, trim, almost boyish-looking 82-year-old wearing a windbreaker over a jaunty yellow polo shirt, would waste his time watching *Friday the 13th* … or *Nightmare on Elm Street*, or any of the other contemporary movies that he calls "slasher" films rather than horror films. "It seems that every new horror film that comes out is trying to be more violent, more bloodthirsty, and, in my opinion, more disgusting than its predecessor," he says in an accent that barely betrays his British upbringing. "I've stopped watching."

Oddly, people have not stopped watching his movies, or the genre films of his older brother, Alex, who died three years ago. A beautifully restored four-disc set of the brothers' work, *Monsters and Madmen*, which features Alex's *The Atomic Submarine* and Richard's well-known movies with horror giant Boris Karloff—*Corridors of Blood* and *The Haunted Strangler*, as well as his science-fiction classic, *First Man Into Space*—still sell briskly on Amazon.com. And horror-movie conventions and genre magazines like *Video Watchdog* still celebrate, and venerate, Gordon, who goes to two or three conventions a year and is greeted like a demigod.

Which is not surprising, since Gordon and his brother started out as genre-movie überfans, and stayed that way their whole lives. "People like François Truffaut, Martin Scorsese and Quentin Tarantino often get the credit," says *Video Watchdog*'s editor and horror-film expert Tim Lucas, "but Richard and Alex Gordon were possibly the very first movie buffs to rise to the occupation of producer." Their love of horror, sci-fi and Western movies gave them an entrée with figures like Lugosi, Karloff and Western star Gene Autry, and ensured that their movies would resonate with a fan base that saw filmed entertainment exactly as the brothers did.

....

So what kind of strange upbringing was responsible for this twin eruption of horror aficionados? Says Gordon, "We were just a perfectly normal English family, living in a suburb of London called Hampstead, not connected in any way with the entertainment business. My father imported plastics into England when they first became popular to use in the United States. The family used to go to the movies every Saturday or Sunday—we had no television then. We got very interested in movies, and then that led to our starting some fan clubs on our own. Alex was particularly interested in Westerns, Gene Autry specifically, and started a Gene Autry fan club. Gradually, that morphed into our careers."

Gordon missed out on college because he was drafted to fight in World War II. "I was in the navy and Alex was in the army. I saw action in the Atlantic on a destroyer named the *Wensleydale*. When we got out in '46, we managed to get jobs in the film industry, on the distribution side in London, but conditions in England at that time were still so harsh — rationing, power cuts — we didn't have the feeling that we were going to get anywhere. My father said, 'Look, if you really want to be in the film business, the only place to do it is in America. Why don't you make the move, go to America, and if it doesn't work you can always come back.' We were both young enough, neither of us was married, we had no other family ties. So in 1947, we emigrated to the United States. I was 21." Gordon has lived and worked in New York ever since.

After a few years toiling for a film importer in New York, Gordon cheekily hung out his own shingle (he was all of 23) and began bringing in B-movies from England, Germany and France, essentially establishing an American market for these offbeat films, creating the model that Harvey and Bob Weinstein used at Miramax, and Robert Shaye at New Line, nearly 30 years later.

But Gordon was still very much a movie fan, and that's how he moved into the next stage of his career. "When Alex and I first came to New York," says Gordon, "one of the ways we had devised to make some extra income was to write articles for British fan magazines and send them back to England. That's how I came to meet actors like Boris Karloff, when he was appearing on the New York stage, or Bela Lugosi, when he was touring in summer stock in *Arsenic and Old Lace*."

....

Lugosi and the Gordon brothers hit it off (Alex soon moved to Los Angeles, where he would spend the rest of his life), in part because the aging Lugosi was eager for appreciation. "His career was going downhill," says Gordon. "He was living in New York, because he felt he could do better on the stage and in television, *The Milton Berle Show*, things like that. He said if I thought I could do something to help his career, he'd be very glad to have me represent him."

In 1951, Gordon was able to set up a stage tour of *Dracula* in England, hoping that if all went well, Lugosi would cross the ocean with the play and conquer Broadway.

It turned out to be the mutual fantasy of a young man with little experience and a former star whose best days were well behind him. "It didn't go well at all," says Gordon. "Bela was already a little too old, and he wasn't in the best of health. The production company that I made the deal with in England was a very cheap touring company and had no money to spend on publicity. They thought that they could just put Bela Lugosi's name on the marquee and everybody would come running to see him in person. The tour closed before it hit the West End of London. The rest of the plan went down the drain."

With virtually no money, Lugosi found himself stranded in London. So Gordon, now all of 25, used his film importing connections to wedge Lugosi into the very British *Old Mother Riley* film series (cheaply made but highly profitable movies starring actor Arthur Lucan in drag, often as a charwoman or laundress who gets herself into humorous trouble). The result, *Old Mother Riley Meets the Vampire*, made Lugosi a tidy $5,000. "Which in those days was a lot more than it is now," says Gordon, "The $5,000 was enough money to get Bela and his wife back to Hollywood after the completion of the picture."

Gordon loved Lugosi as only a fan could, and wished he had been able to do more for him. "He was a very dignified man, who came from a very good family in Hungary," he says. "He was a matinee idol on the stage in Hungary, he did Romeo, he did Shake-speare, everything that you would expect. At an early stage in his career he decided to leave Hungary for Germany, where he worked for a while in the German cinema, then he came to the United States. He was a real gentleman. There was sadness on Alex's and my part that the circumstances didn't bring us together earlier, when we might have done more for him and he might have done more for us."

Gordon spent the mid-1950s importing movies and coproducing B-movies with hard-boiled action actors like Zachary Scott, Pat O'Brien and Rod Cameron, which were released by companies like Warner Brothers and Columbia. But his fan-magazine writing soon landed him another opportunity. He had interviewed Boris Karloff for a British fan magazine in the early 1950s, when Karloff was starring in the Broadway plays *The Linden Tree* and, later, *The Shop at Sly Corner*. "We struck up a sort of friendship," says Gordon. "Boris maintained an apartment at the Dakota for when he was appearing in New York, so we got together from time to time." Clearly, Karloff saw Gordon as not just a fan, but a charming and capable person who might someday really make something of his passion.

"One day," says Gordon, "Boris handed me a story called *Stranglehold*, which had been written especially for him by a screenwriter in England, Jan Read, who was fairly well-known, and he said to me, 'Why don't you read this and see what you think of it? If you think it's something that you could set up in England for production, I'd be willing to come over and do it and you can use my name.' That was a wonderful offer, and it's what really got me started. It became *The Haunted Strangler*."

The Haunted Strangler, like *Corridors of Blood*, which Gordon would produce later with Karloff, was a beautifully shot and acted horror film set in mid-19th century England. In the film, Karloff starts off as a novelist investigating a 20-year-old murder case; in *Corridors*, he is a crusading doctor so keen to find an effective anesthetic for the surgery he performs that he experiments on himself. In both movies, his character begins with great dignity, making his eventual ghoulish transformation that much more effective. Gordon feels strongly that Karloff's gentility and even vulnerability were qualities that set him off from other horror-film actors. "You can trace that right back to the original *Frankenstein*," he says. "He made a pathetic figure out of the Frankenstein monster, not just a hulk with no background. And throughout most of his career he played that kind of a role."

....

Gordon sees clear differences between his two horror heroes. Unlike the more complex Karloff, "Bela Lugosi was inclined to play roles of outright villainy, and really based his career on his success in *Dracula*," he says. Off camera, Karloff was also quite different from the brooding, temperamental Lugosi. "Boris Karloff was a typical English country gentleman," says Gordon. "He was interested in gardening, he played cricket, he was a part of the British community in Hollywood. Karloff was a wonderful man. A gentleman, he was kind, and he was quite astute about his own career; he handled it extremely well. He had been on Broadway, had been on television, he did recordings, and he had a very, very successful career."

Gordon believes that the great horror-film actors "have the ability to take what they are doing seriously, as it is intended by the producer and director, and give it some dignity, no matter what the role forces them to do. It's their ability and plasticity." And Gordon feels these qualities have nothing to do with the age of the actor. "You see it in Christopher Lee," he says, "who is also in *Corridors of Blood*." Yes, that Christopher Lee! Gordon managed to snag the young unknown for what had originally been the bit part of the fiendish Resurrection Joe, who happily smothers his victims, right before Lee's *The Curse of Frankenstein* came out and made an international splash. That film made Lee the successor to Lugosi and Karloff as not only Frankenstein but Dracula and The Mummy as well. Lee, of course, is now best known as Scaramanga in *The Man with the Golden Gun*, Count Dooku in the second *Star Wars* trilogy, and the evil Saruman in the three *Lord of the Rings* films.

Gordon clearly feels that even as a young horror wannabee, Lee knew where he was going. "Lee's a fine actor," he says. "He was convinced, and of course he turned out to be right, that when *The Curse of Frankenstein* was released, he would be a major star."

After producing two of his best-known films, the 1977 remake of *The Cat and the Canary* and the futuristic, sci-fi horror *Inseminoid* in 1980, Gordon decided that production and marketing costs had gotten too high, so he simply got out of the production end. But he had had the extraordinary foresight to make sure that after a period of time, the rights to his films that the major companies had distributed reverted to him. "When I started in the late 1950s, when I made my first deal with MGM for worldwide distribution of *The Haunted Strangler* and my first science-fiction picture, *Fiend without a Face*, I was able to negotiate a deal," he says. "Because there was no such thing as home movies or anything like that, I got all the material and copyrights back."

Gordon still does a brisk business exploiting his vintage horror pictures, some 50 years after some of them were made. "I also represent certain other companies and help them with their international sales," he says, "and I'm representing companies placing their films here in the United States. I work with home video distributors Criterion Collection, Kino International and First Run Features, and with cable television networks like Turner Classic Movies, the Sundance Channel and others."

Sitting in his well-tended office, Gordon is surrounded by DVDs of the films he made that grew out of his love for all things horror way back in Hampstead. Having lived in New York for the past 60 years, he sounds very much like a New Yorker, albeit a very dignified one. He is, after all, still a British subject. "I have a British passport and never became an American citizen," he says. "During the years I was in production, I spent a lot of time in England, but I never wanted to go back to live there. I decided New York was the place for me. I have what they used to call a green card, and I've lived quite happily here." (Which puts him, no doubt, in a rarefied group of extremely long-term expatriates.)

Gordon never married and has no children of his own, so his communion with a younger generation is through the kind of fan magazines he once wrote for and through the horror-movie conventions. "They usually show one or another of my films, and have me do question-and-answer sessions with the audience," he says. "I sign autographs, all the usual things that go with these horror conventions. It's a lot of fun for me. I love being able to talk about movies, especially the old movies. It certainly gives one a good feeling. It always surprises me what a long life these films have, and how they keep coming back." ≈

❧

Crashing the
Boys' Club

....

by LESLIE BENNETTS
illustrations by MICHELE CARLSON

SHE DOESN'T WEAR HER TRADEMARK LEOPARD COAT ANY MORE — SOME
activist who didn't realize it was decades old might throw red paint on it — and that
helmet of blond hair is silver now. But Muriel Siebert couldn't honestly be said to have
toned down her flamboyant image. At 76, she has two purple leather suits and she still
wears both of them, as she does her custom-made black polka-dot leather jacket.

Although Siebert's sartorial style was always as bold as she is, "the first woman of
finance" never needed arresting clothes to attract attention. When she began her career
more than a half-century ago, it was unheard of for a woman to breach the all-male
precincts of financial power — let alone barge in with the irrepressible chutzpah that she

brought to the task. As a Wall Street pioneer, she spent many years as both the first and the only female in a groundbreaking series of important positions, where her mere presence was more than sufficient to draw all eyes.

Even today, Muriel Siebert & Co. is still the only woman-owned New York Stock Exchange (NYSE) brokerage firm with a national presence. Visitors are greeted with an array of testimonials to Siebert's illustrious resume as soon as they enter the waiting room, where the walls are hung with front-page newspaper stories and other documents chronicling her career, starting with a quaint 1967 newspaper ad touting her services as the first female member of the exchange.

The decor inside Siebert's office provides further evidence of her enduring influence. "That's my presidential wall," she says, waving a hand at the array of photographs featuring Siebert with almost every president of the last 40 years, from Richard Nixon, Jimmy Carter and Ronald Reagan ("My favorite!") to George Bush and Bill Clinton, along with a framed personal note from George W. Bush thanking Siebert for coming to the White House in 2001 to discuss the state of America's economy "in such a candid way."

Looking back on decades of achievement, Siebert is particularly proud of having maintained an unblemished reputation in an arena where various forms of malfeasance have landed others in prison and brought down major companies. The financial distress now roiling many sectors is almost enough to make her nostalgic for the good old days, sexist though they may have been.

"I've been in the business a long time, and we've done things the clean way," she says. "When I came into the industry, a lot of people really didn't want me. But there was a code of ethics I thought was magnificent. Your word was your bond. If you weren't honest and you took advantage of someone on a trade, word would get out and nobody would do business with you. I took pride because my customers trusted both my ability and my integrity."

These days, however, dire headlines attest to a widespread deterioration of moral standards as well as sound financial practices. "The industry has changed. You wonder, How the hell did these banks get in all that trouble? Some of those guys belonged in jail," Siebert says. "A lot of the new products are not designed with the customer's best interest at heart. There are a lot of very sophisticated products that are not designed to give the individual a fair shot. In some cases, firms have made billions of dollars—and now they're losing it."

She blames simple greed for the trend toward cutting corners and compromising professional ethics. "The money is so vast; it's too much of a temptation to a lot of people," she says.

But for Siebert, there were always more important considerations; as a pioneer, she held herself to different standards altogether. "I think that, as a role model, you have an obligation," she says. "I didn't need all the money in the world; I didn't have to be the largest. I just wanted to make sure that, as the first woman member, I had the cleanest record, as far as ethics and morals were concerned."

The daughter of a Cleveland dentist, Siebert cites two formative influences in shaping her destiny: a noteworthy talent for numbers and the palpable unhappiness of her mother, which precluded any interest Siebert might otherwise have had in becoming a homemaker who devoted herself to raising a family.

"My mother loved her children, but she was totally frustrated," Siebert says. "She had a God-given voice, and she had offers to go onstage, but nice Jewish girls didn't do that. She was a frustrated artist who stayed home until my father died of cancer at 52 and we needed money, when she got a job as a saleswoman in a department store."

Although Siebert recoiled from the "feminine mystique" that entrapped her mother, exciting alternatives were not readily apparent in that era. But Siebert was never one to follow the conventional path. Even as a college student at Western Reserve, which

"For nearly ten years I could say that it was 1,365 men and me.

That's more than being delightfully outnumbered."

is now Case Western Reserve University, she flouted the rules with the kind of blithe insouciance that later made her such a notorious maverick on Wall Street.

"I wasn't going to class; I was playing bridge," admits Siebert, who never graduated. "I didn't have any goals. The one thing I learned at college was that numbers jumped off a page to me. If you ask me to spell something, I might have to stop and think about it. But I can look at a page of numbers, and if something's out of line, it'll pop out and say hello to me. I could skip classes, take the test and get an A. It's nothing I had to cultivate; it's a natural aptitude."

Her older sister inadvertently supplied the launching pad for Siebert's career. "I had been to New York once before, on a vacation that included a tour of the balcony of the New York Stock Exchange," she reports. "I said, 'This looks exciting!'" When her sister got divorced, Siebert decided to join her in Manhattan. "I had a couch to sleep on," she says with a shrug. "I came to New York with $500 and a used Studebaker."

Her fortunes quickly improved, thanks to shrewd instincts and the ability to learn fast. "I applied to Merrill Lynch for a job," she recalls with a sly smile. "They said, 'College degree?' I said, 'No.' They said, 'No job.' So I applied to Bache & Co. They said, 'College degree?' I said, 'Yes.' And I got a job as a research trainee at $65 a week." She grins triumphantly.

As her areas of expertise, Siebert was assigned the airlines and radio, television and motion pictures — all fast-growing industries in the mid-1950s. The explosion of television soon inspired an epiphany when Siebert realized that old films — a theretofore unappreciated asset of the motion picture companies — would develop a value on television. "So I wrote a report," she says — a prescient contribution that landed her not only a new and better job as a securities analyst, but also the business of grateful clients who had made money from her insight.

She quickly developed a taste for the thrill of wielding power. "That's a pretty feeling, to say you can study something and people will follow up on it and they're backing that up with real money," she says. "And this was not Muriel Siebert saying something that had the backing of Goldman Sachs; in order to be paid more equally, I had to go to small firms."

But the entrenched sexism of the financial world presented formidable obstacles to the kind of recognition she sought. "I was being paid half to three-quarters of what the men were being paid," she says. Indeed, it was Siebert's rancor over ongoing sex discrimination that ultimately provided the impetus for her historic move to impose gender integration on the New York Stock Exchange.

"I asked Jerry Tsai, who was running the Manhattan Fund, what large firm I could go to where I would be paid equally," she reports. "He said, 'Don't be ridiculous; you won't. Buy a seat and work for yourself.' I said, 'Don't *you* be ridiculous!' They had never accepted a woman. He said, 'I don't think there's a law against it.' So I took the constitution of the New York Stock Exchange home and studied it, and I said, 'I think I qualify.' It took me a while to make it happen, but I did."

Siebert was turned down by nine of the first 10 men she asked to sponsor her application, but on December 28, 1967, she became the first woman member of the NYSE, making front-page news and sending shock waves throughout the financial industry. "For nearly 10 years, I could say that it was 1,365 men and me," she says dryly. "That's more than being delightfully outnumbered."

When asked how her male colleagues treated her, she grimaces. "Like shit," she says. "The day I got the seat, they handed every man who was a new member a scroll and a badge. The scroll must be prominently displayed, and the badge is worn on the floor of the exchange. But they didn't give one to me, and that crushed me. It hurt me deeply. It said that they didn't want me. I had to threaten to get mine."

Siebert prevailed, but her growing success remained difficult for many men to accept, particularly in a profession where money provides an all-too-concrete means of keeping score. Although she says she came "close a few times," she has never married.

"If you're on Wall Street and the man's on Wall Street, there's an underlying competition about money," she explains. "I was making very good money by the time I bought the seat—half a million dollars a year, which was real money then—and that makes it tough. A man has to be very secure within himself to be able to handle with pride a successful woman—somebody who's hitting the newspapers, somebody who you walk into a room and people know who she is. I should have gotten involved with a doctor who was doing research or something, but I was meeting people in my world, where there was direct competition based on money."

Notwithstanding the personal cost of her success, however, there is no mistaking the exhilaration Siebert felt at its rewards—and the relish she took in measuring her progress. "I was earning as much as the presidents of companies, and I was enjoying it," she says. "I did some things no woman had done, and I was proud because I had done this. I commanded respect."

As feminism gained momentum in the late 1960s and early 1970s, the barriers to women's equality continued to topple. Although Siebert, unlike many feminist leaders, is a lifelong Republican, she wholeheartedly supported the goals of the women's movement. "I respected what they were doing, and I became active. I joined almost all the organizations," she says.

She also continued to test the limits of social and institutional change. Siebert shook up the financial system again, in 1975, when a new federal law abolished fixed commissions for brokers. Siebert promptly announced that Muriel Siebert & Co. would become a discount commission house.

Once again, the men controlling the levers of power reacted with hostility; Siebert's longtime clearinghouse dropped her. She managed to finagle a 30-day extension from the Securities and Exchange Commission and signed on with another clearinghouse.

Two years later, Governor Hugh Carey appointed Siebert as New York's first female superintendent of banking. She served five years before resigning in 1982 to run unsuccessfully for New York State's Republican Senate nomination.

Although she barreled through one gender barrier after another, she never down-played her femininity in order to function in a man's world. To the contrary—Siebert reveled in posing for glamorous magazine photographs like the one that showed her as a well-coiffed blond in a leopard coat, leaning against her own silver Mercedes 350SL. Her financial success earned her an enviable lifestyle; over the years, she lived at such prestigious Manhattan addresses as Sutton Place and River House and bought homes in La Costa and East Hampton. She also took on familial responsibilities, assuming the lifelong financial support of her mother and her sister. These days, Siebert has a condo in Southampton and another home in Palm Beach.

Despite such quintessential emblems of life at the top, however, Siebert has always seen herself in far more down-to-earth terms. She is blunt and plainspoken, and when asked about the qualities that facilitated her success, she replies, "I'm a Midwesterner, and Midwesterners are pretty tough, honest people. They look you in the eye; your word is your bond. I did not look or sound like a New Yorker."

Today her silver hair is tousled, she is clad in casual slacks and a shirt, and she appears to be wearing no makeup, although her fingernails sport a fire-engine-red manicure. In conversation, she is terse and to the point. Near her desk is a television screen with the sound turned down, and she seems to absorb the financial news unspooling silently across the screen as naturally as breathing. In midsentence about another subject, she mutters suddenly, "The Dow's up 115!" and then continues with her previous train of thought.

Despite her advancing years, Siebert remains chairwoman and chief executive officer as well as the founder of Muriel Siebert & Co., a discount brokerage firm with offices in four states—four in Florida, one in New Jersey and one in Beverly Hills, in addition to the New York office. The company, which does $30 million to $40 million in business every year, has some 150 employees.

"We're smaller than we used to be, but I want the privilege of doing the kind of business I want to do," says Siebert, whose office floor is littered with dog toys. The company's resident mascot is her long-haired Chihuahua, Monster Girl, who accompanies Siebert to work but spends most of the day sleeping, awakening occasionally to deliver a fierce volley of yaps before lapsing back into torpor.

Unlike Monster Girl, Siebert herself has no interest in taking it easy, let alone retiring from the fray. "I would get bored if I sat and did nothing," she says. "I like my mind to work."

Women's advancement continues to be a priority, and she remains active in many organizations, including the New York Women's Forum, of which she is a founder and former president. As she surveys the financial world today, she sees considerable progress despite lingering impediments. "There has been a lot of improvement, but it's slow," she says. "On Wall Street, you don't have a woman who is head of any major firm. I think men have changed, to a degree. They are less resentful. When you get married today, you need two salaries, so men are very supportive of a wife's moving ahead. They respect the woman's paycheck. The 'little lady' is not just working because she wants pin money. They're working because if they want a certain standard of life, they have to."

As Siebert correctly notes, the majority of American families now require two incomes to supply the same middle-class standard of living that the typical male breadwinner could provide with one salary when she entered the workforce. Since then, women have penetrated most of the men-only bastions of power that characterized her youth, and many have followed in her footsteps to build formidable careers throughout the financial sector.

But Siebert's restless intelligence has never stopped searching for new frontiers, and one of her brainstorms commands an increasing proportion of her attention these days. Ever since she was superintendent of banking, Siebert has been deeply concerned about the financial incompetence of many young people, and a decade ago, she decided to do something about it.

"I saw kids who were bankrupt at 22," she says. "No one was teaching young people how to manage what they earned; they weren't learning it in school, and they didn't know how to handle it. We wouldn't have had the current mortgage mess to this degree if people had known what they were signing."

Siebert decided that high schools ought to be teaching financial literacy to their students, and she set up a meeting with Rudy Crew, then New York City's chancellor of the Board of Education, to propose such a curriculum. As she explored the possibilities, the stories she heard were poignant, indeed. Teachers not only told her about young people who had to be bailed out of credit card debt, but about some of their graduates who were so ignorant they thought thieves must be stealing money from their paychecks, because they didn't know that taxes were taken out of their earnings.

Working with professionals in curriculum development, Siebert came up with the Personal Finance Program, which is administered through the nonprofit Muriel F. Siebert Foundation. It's been implemented in 280 schools in 10 states, and Siebert is hoping to make it a required course nationwide. She also wants to expand it to reach younger students.

Notwithstanding the number and variety of other achievements gilding her resume, Siebert now regards the finance program as one of her most important accomplishments.

Siebert's focus on information and empowerment reflects an unshakable belief in the basic homespun virtues — and their rewards. On one hand, she wears a glittering red-white-and-blue American flag ring. "I bought it on a corner the week after 9/11," she reports. "It cost $5. I had a real one made, but it doesn't sparkle the way the fake one does, so I'm still wearing it."

As the ring attests, Siebert remains a passionate booster of the United States and the opportunities it represents. She is herself a remarkable example of America's ongoing progress in expanding women's rights, and she has never forgotten to appreciate the ethos of social justice that made her success possible.

"I believe in this country," she says. "You have to be realistic, but if you're willing to work, this is still the best country there is. You can do whatever you want to do if you have the talent." ≈

View Finder

by J.G. DWYER

illustrations by PETER JAMES FIELD

THE YEAR WAS 1963, THE EXACT MONTH NOW UNCERTAIN, BUT ALL THE other details are still pinned to the memory of Ken Heyman, photographer.

Margaret Mead had summoned him to dinner at a fine French restaurant just off Central Park West in Manhattan. That, Heyman knew, meant it was important. And not just because it was an evening with Mead, the anthropologist, author and perhaps the world's most famous woman scientist.

He had known Mead for nearly a decade, since his days in the 1950s as a student at Columbia University, and he occasionally accompanied her on field trips to take pictures. Those journeys always began with a minimalist phone call from "the Mead."

"You'd pick up the phone and hear her voice saying, 'Waverly Place,' which was where she lived," Heyman says. "Then she'd say, 'six o'clock, Thursday,' and she'd hang up. Never said hello or good-bye."

This time, though, Mead wanted to meet with him at Café des Artistes, her favorite restaurant. "That meant," Heyman says, "that we would have a serious talk."

At dinner, beneath the restaurant's famous murals, Mead laid out her plan and Heyman's part in it.

"I'd like to do a book on families," she said.

She would set out to conduct a sweeping exploration of family structures around the globe, and she wanted Heyman to take the pictures. The visual narrative and her written accounts would run alongside each other.

"That would be marvelous," Heyman told her.

He asked a few practical questions. They would split the proceeds 50-50. The publisher would cover their expenses.

A few days later, though, Heyman found out what the trip would really cost him. He had recently become a full member of Magnum, the photo agency owned by the premier photographers in the world, so he met with the manager to let him know that he would be traveling and unavailable for months to take on any new assignments.

"Ken, you have to choose between doing the book with Margaret Mead or working with Magnum," the manager told him. "We have to have money coming in. This is a cooperative." That would have been a sobering moment for any photographer, but especially for Heyman.

Every age has its great photojournalists, admired for their vision, their courage and their execution. For about 25 years, from the 1940s through the early 1960s, photographers owned the day. Television was an embryonic medium, not yet a full member of the American family. The world's premier communicator of news and culture was *Life* magazine, then at its most muscular, selling 13 million copies a week. It occupied that space because its pictures were unparalleled, and it functioned as the grand stage of photography, publishing the work of Margaret Bourke-White, Gordon Parks, Robert Capa and Alfred Eisenstaedt.

Into this era strode Ken Heyman—born to an affluent New York family, the lumbering boy who made the high school football team not for any talent but for his size, an indifferent soldier during his two years in the army and, upon his return, a mediocre student. "I was a kid," he said, "with no success in my whole life." At Columbia University, he spent little time in the classroom, and began prowling the city for pictures. He also landed in a class taught by Mead, with a requirement that the students apply the techniques of anthropological observation to New York City. For his final paper, Heyman turned in a series of incisive photographs from a settlement house in Harlem. Mead knew that pictures were essential to the records of life made by anthropologists, every bit as important as written accounts of ritual behavior.

"Ken Heyman," Mead would later say, "photographs relationships."

A year or so after he graduated, Mead asked him to come with her to Bali for the first of many brief field trips. And in the meantime, Heyman—shocked by graduation from college and the need to confront daily life—had started to get work with *Life*. He

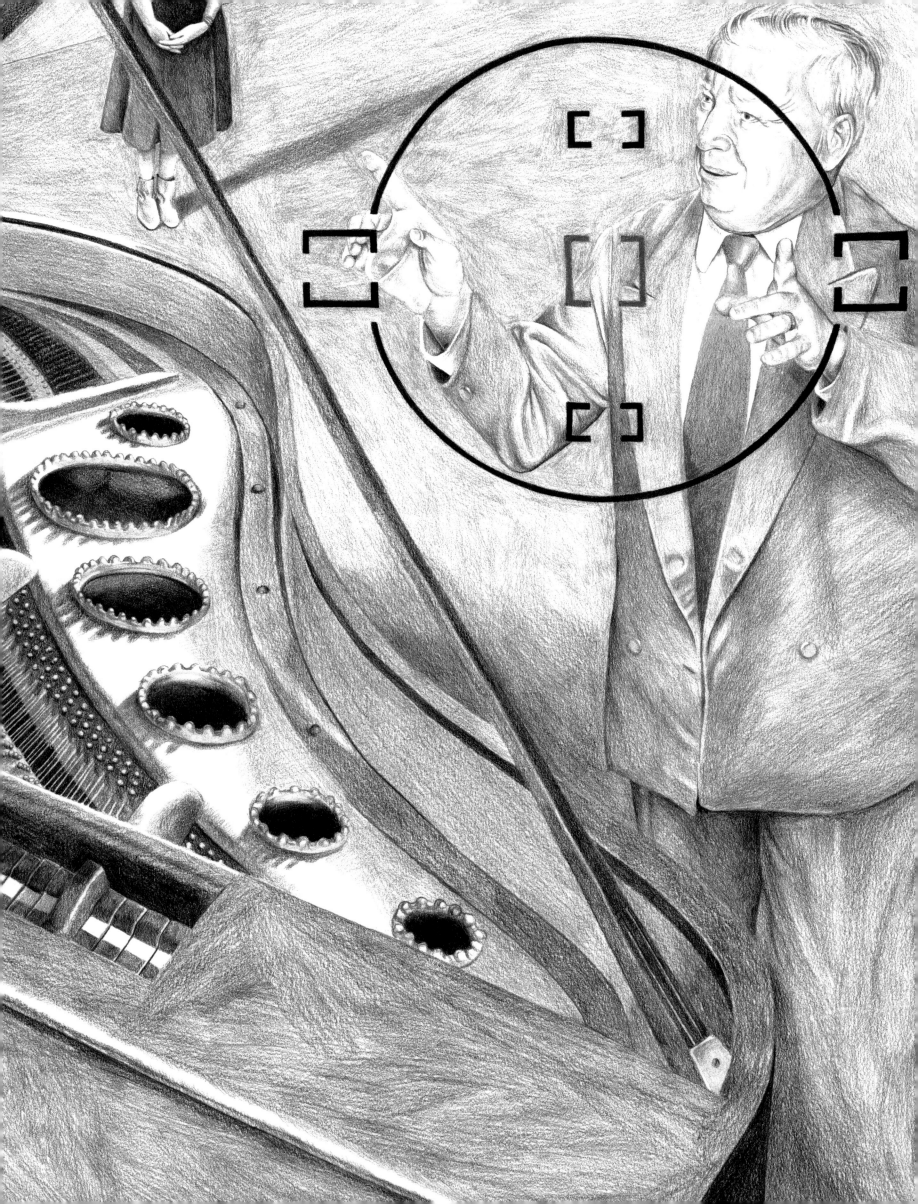

sent in a series of pictures on people who spent parts of each day on the park benches in the little traffic islands that run along Broadway on Manhattan's Upper West Side. More than portraits, his pictures tracked lives crossing, like wires. The picture editors at *Life* noticed. He got one assignment. Then another.

Within a couple of years, he had made himself into one of the country's top photographers. He shot an iconic picture of Marilyn Monroe and Arthur Miller on their wedding day. At a bullfight in Spain, he spied Pablo Picasso in the stands across the ring and strolled past, camera in hand, firing off one frame. On a $20 bet with his brother, he talked his way into Ernest Hemingway's villa in Cuba, ignored a profane, hostile greeting, and took pictures of the macho writer cuddling with one of his cats.

No one had seen a picture of Hemingway like that before; he posed as a man of action, of safaris and war and adventure, not as some plump, bearded man attached to his kitty.

"I didn't think I had talent," Heyman says. "I didn't think of it in terms of that. All I knew was they kept hiring me and reassigning me."

He had enough work to set up his own studio on Manhattan's East Side—and even managed to get a struggling young artist to paint its bathroom for $400. He wound up with a tropical tree running from the floor to the ceiling, butterflies along the wall and a calico cat on the toilet seat. The artist, a man of wispy hair and sure strokes, was named Andy Warhol. (Heyman later took a picture of Warhol sitting on a faux throne in the artist's studio for the first book on pop art. And many years on, when there was a major sale of Warhol work, Heyman remembers thinking: *I wish I had saved that toilet seat.*)

Not only was *Life* magazine giving him regular work; then Magnum came calling, a gateway to more assignments, more prestige.

"And I chose Margaret," Heyman says. "She was a wise woman. She knew everything. And she made sense. She became my teacher. Bali is a beautiful place, where the people are extraordinarily beautiful. She didn't just go to Bali, she went to the most remote place, the other side of a volcano, no roads, and the people were actually uglier than most Balinese. Whether it was Mexico, Sicily, wherever, in each case, she wanted the most remote place, that was influenced the least."

The work catapulted him as far from the worlds of Marilyn Monroe and Hemingway as a photographer could get. Heyman and Mead came back with a 208-page book of pictures and narratives, *Family*. It included 200 of Heyman's photographs, and eight chapters by Mead. *The New York Times Book Review* called it "a handsome picture primer of humanity's basic group." It was nominated for a Pulitzer prize, and the Book of the Month Club made it a main selection, the first book of photography to have that distinction. It sold over 250,000 copies.

"It made my career," Heyman said.

He went back to Bali in 1976 with some of the photographs, and Heyman took pictures of people looking at the old pictures, trying to find themselves or their families. Those pictures were turned into a giant mural that Mead hung at the entryway to a retrospective exhibition of her work in the American Museum of Natural History.

For Heyman, his photography and his eye continued to be sought after the *Family* book. He was commissioned to spend a month with the composer and conductor Leonard Bernstein, and traveled with his family to a rented villa on the Mediterranean.

One morning, Bernstein sat with him at breakfast. "I'd like you to have dinner tonight with us," Bernstein said.

"Sure," Heyman said, thinking—*what's the big deal, I have dinner with you every night*.

"We're having special guests," Bernstein continued. "Charlie Chaplin and his family."

That was special: Chaplin was living in a peculiar state of exile from the United States, living a reclusive life in Switzerland with his wife, Oona O'Neill Chaplin, the daughter of the playwright Eugene O'Neill, and their children.

"So I want you to come to dinner, but not your cameras," Bernstein said.

Heyman agreed. That night, seated alongside Bernstein and Chaplin, he watched as the maestro drew out Chaplin. "Lenny knew how to make people emote," Heyman recalled. "You had two performers trying to outdo each other, one topping the other."

When dinner was over, Bernstein turned to Chaplin.

"Charlie, would you play 'Limelight'?" he asked.

Chaplin had composed the theme to *Limelight* himself, to accompany one of his greatest movies. He sat down at the piano and played it.

Heyman watched as Bernstein then slid onto the bench that Chaplin had just vacated.

"He took two navel oranges, and he rolled them over the black notes—it was a musician's trick—and out came this beautiful music," Heyman recalled. "So Charlie has to top this one."

Chaplin asked Bernstein, "Do you have the music for *La Traviata*?"

Bernstein opened the piano bench, found the score and, instructed by Chaplin, began to play.

Then, Heyman said, Chaplin opened his mouth.

"He sang the male and female parts, acting it out. He knew it completely. He's an older Chaplin, but still."

Heyman sidled up to Bernstein's wife, Felicia. "My cameras are in the closet—what do you think? Could I photograph?"

"Don't ask me, go ask Oona," she replied.

Heyman whispered to Oona.

"Oh, I think Charlie would love it," she said.

Heyman recalls, "Within 30 seconds, I was there shooting away."

The performance was a showstopper, the end of the evening.

"They were leaving, and I happened to be in front of his two beautiful teenage daughters, and I said to them, 'Oh, it must have been so wonderful, growing up with a father that entertains like this.'

"And they looked like they'd seen a ghost, and they said, 'We've never seen him do this before, only in the old movies.'"

And in Ken Heyman's pictures of that night in Italy, you can see, just over Charlie Chaplin's shoulder, a daughter looking on in stark amazement, her father reborn before her eyes as comic genius, hat in hand. Once again, as Margaret Mead said, Ken Heyman had photographed a relationship. ≈

ARTIST OF PERSUASION

by ERIC POOLEY
illustrations by MATS GUSTAFSON

SK MOST GLOBAL-WARMING ACTIVISTS HOW THEY GOT INVOLVED
in the climate issue and you'll hear about polar-bear moments: encounters with the
natural world that made them suddenly, viscerally grasp the urgency of the threat. For
some, the moment came during a walk through a mountain forest destroyed by pine
beetles—a marauding army of bugs, once kept at bay by extremely cold winters, that
has killed millions of trees from Colorado to British Columbia. For others, it was the
sight of glaciers vanishing or permafrost sagging or daffodils blooming in January or,
yes, polar bears stranded on a chunk of floating, melting Arctic sea ice.

Pose the same question to Theodore Kheel—the legendary New York power broker and labor mediator who has devoted the past two decades to environmental work—and you learn two things. First, Kheel's moment of awakening took place before most people had heard of global warming. Second, it happened not in the wilds of nature but on West 52nd Street in Manhattan, amid the gleaming wood and polished brass of the "21" Club. Which makes perfect sense, because Ted Kheel, still dapper and urbane at 94, is both a quintessential New Yorker and a man ahead of his time: a rapid-fire thinker and talker and doer, an adviser to mayors and settler of mammoth disputes, a champion of mass transit and the city's surprisingly fragile ecosystem.

Kheel's green awakening happened in 1991, as he was attending a luncheon at the landmark restaurant, where he had been a regular for a decade or more. A beautiful woman at his table—someone he'd never met before—asked him a question.

"Are you going to Rio?"

Kheel chuckled. "Why would I go to Rio?"

"For the Earth Summit."

"What is the Earth Summit?"

The woman turned out to be an artist named Maria Cooper Janis, the daughter of actor Gary Cooper. She explained that the Earth Summit was an important United Nations conference that would draw leaders from all over the world—172 nations, as it turned out—in an attempt to reconcile two goals that were on a collision course: global economic growth and environmental survival. The sustainable development movement was being born, and Kheel was immediately captivated by it. Here was conflict on a grand scale—economic progress versus the fate of the earth—and he had spent his entire career reconciling the seemingly irreconcilable. Besides, he was ready for a new challenge. He was 77 years old and restless—every bit as restless and driven, in fact, as he had always been.

Born in Brooklyn in 1914 and raised in Manhattan, Kheel has resolved, by his own count, many thousands of labor disputes over the years. He was executive director of the National War Labor Board during World War II, which quelled imbroglios that might have hindered the war effort, and was New York City's arbitrator of transit disputes for 33 years, huddling with mayors William O'Dwyer, Robert F. Wagner and John Lindsay (a period of insider-ism that ended with the election of Ed Koch—Koch and Kheel loathed each other). He commanded the front pages and brokered solutions to some of the greatest labor-management fights of the century: the East Coast longshoremen's strike of 1962, which crippled ports along the Eastern Seaboard; the New York newspaper strike of 1963, which shut down the city's dailies for 114 days; the national railroad strike of 1964, which President Lyndon Johnson called him in to mediate. No wonder *The New York Times* has called him "the most influential industrial peacemaker in New York City in the last half-century" or that *BusinessWeek* crowned him the "master locksmith of deadlock bargaining."

When he learned about the Earth Summit in Rio, Kheel saw a chance to help break this global deadlock. "At the time, I was sympathetic to environmental concerns, but I could in no way be called an environmentalist," he says, wearing seersucker and sitting at a massive mahogany desk in his East 55th Street office, a glass wall looking out on the city behind him. "But when I discovered that this U.N. conference represented a conflict between two goals, both of which the U.N. was promoting—protection of the environment and development of the global economy—I saw that it was a classic dispute. So I got involved."

Rio turned out to be a tremendously important conference. It established the U.N. Framework Convention on Climate Change (a treaty signed by the first President Bush), which led directly to the Kyoto Protocol (a treaty scorned by the second President

Bush and now ratified by every industrialized country except the United States). But in the months leading up to Rio, the conference organizers told Kheel they needed a higher public profile, so he set about giving them one. He reached out to his friends in the media and asked a friend and client, the great artist Robert Rauschenberg, to create a piece of art for the Earth Summit. Rauschenberg came up with a dramatic painting — a rainforest canopy rendered in cool greens and blues, desiccated trees splashed in orange; a baby fussing in a stroller under a small red umbrella; an anguished Atlas holding up a celestial sphere. With the proceeds from the sale of the prints, Kheel then started a newspaper called *The Earth Times* and created an organization called the Earth Pledge Foundation to promote a simple, difficult promise: making the earth a hospitable home for present and future generations. Rauschenberg, who died recently, titled this painting "Last Turn — Your Turn," a call for individual responsibility and action that Kheel says "grows each day in relevance and significance. Bob's foresight was typically brilliant."

So was Kheel's. In fact, the politicians and policymakers who are trying to solve the climate problem could profit from his 1999 book, *The Keys to Conflict Resolution*, which suggests that "the gentle art of losing face … may some day save the human race." In the book, Kheel describes the essential early steps needed to resolve any conflict: defining and framing the issues in dispute, gathering and assessing the facts. When it comes to the climate issue, he believes, these early steps went awry. Climate skeptics managed to delay action for ten years by arguing that the basic science wasn't settled — an argument that a few are still trying to make today, even though climatologists and national academies of science throughout the world all agree that global warming is a clear and present danger. Because of the preponderance of evidence, the debate in the U.S. has finally shifted from science to politics and economics — from whether the threat is real to what we should do about it. Now the conflict is between those who say that dealing with the crisis by reducing emissions will cripple our economy, and those who say that it can be solved with new alternative-energy technologies—which would have the side benefit of freeing us from dependence on foreign oil. There's no more important debate going on in America now. So, of course, Kheel is a part of it.

"It has been said that you can't argue with a fact, you can only be ignorant of it," he says. But the climate skeptics are indeed arguing vociferously about the facts—so how does Kheel think this conflict will be resolved? "I try to be optimistic," he says, "but that's a pretty hard question to answer when the president of the United States is not responding with any urgency to the issue. Think about where we are: the Kyoto Protocol has been adopted by every developed country in the world except the United States. So what do you do about that? It becomes a political matter."

He says these words fiercely, and his eyes are burning—midway through his tenth decade, Kheel's engagement with the world remains so passionate that someone half a century younger might envy it. It's the summer of 2008, shortly before the political conventions that will begin the final phase of the upcoming U.S. presidential election, and Kheel is heartened that both major candidates support mandatory reductions in greenhouse gas emissions. He's a Barack Obama supporter—and, as it happens, he had a small hand not only in making the Obama candidacy possible, but also in making the candidate himself possible. In 1959, Kheel became a founding member of the African-American Students Foundation, which over the next few years airlifted 779 young African scholars to the U.S. One of those students was a Kenyan named Barack Obama, who attended the University of Hawaii, met and married a woman named Ann Dunham, and fathered a son before leaving Dunham and eventually returning to Kenya. Kheel hopes to see that son become the next president. "My life is a series of coincidences," he says with a mixture of satisfaction and wonder. "They have propelled me."

Kheel believes each side will have to climb down from cherished positions.

"You can't have everything you want. You're not going to get the other side to agree to commit suicide."

He speaks more slowly these days—the rat-a-tat delivery is a thing of the past—but still with great precision, and his gaze remains steady and direct. Getting around is problematic; he has been battling spinal stenosis for years, so his back is crooked, stiff and painful. He resisted using a cane for as long as possible, but now propels himself with the help of a walker. "I don't play squash anymore," he says stubbornly, "but I'm still feeling good." In 2004, shortly after the death of his wife of 66 years, journalist and civic leader Ann Sunstein Kheel, he decided to move out of their home in the gracious, leafy Riverdale section of the Bronx, where they'd raised five daughters and a son. He keeps an apartment in Manhattan to be closer to his office, where he still conducts business nearly every day. Retirement is not an option. "I will be retired someday," he admits, "but it won't be voluntary." There's still so much to be done.

The ultimate lesson of Kheel's work is this: To forge a compromise, you must get each side to understand the costs and constraints governing the other side. "Robert Burns, the Scottish poet, wished for the gift of seeing ourselves as others see us. But with apologies to Burns, there's an addendum that's just as important in negotiation: seeing the other guy as he sees himself. Know what he needs and why, and what it will cost him to give you what you want. To get your problem solved, it helps to solve his problem."

That's crucial to climate debate, since environmentalists sometimes fail to understand the constraints the business community is under—the electric utilities, for instance, need to keep the lights on for millions of customers. To find a compromise that solves the problem without damaging the economy, Kheel believes each side will have to climb down from cherished positions. "You can't have everything you want," Kheel says. "You're not going to get the other side to agree to commit suicide."

Kheel has spent the past few years building institutions to help forge the great compromise that he believes will ultimately save the planet. The Nurture Nature

Foundation, which sprang out of his Earth Pledge organization, recently gave $1 million to Pace University to create a center for the resolution of so-called "environmental interest disputes"—conflicts in which no laws are broken, yet there's grave societal harm. (Global warming is a handy example.) A few years ago, his other philanthropy, Nurture New York's Nature, gave $1 million to the City University of New York for a sustainable development curriculum. And Kheel still loves to inject himself into New York's public policy debates. Last year, 42 years after he landed on the front pages of all the New York papers by calling for a doubling of the city's bridge-and-tunnel tolls to finance mass transit (Robert Moses himself called the idea "illegal," but it happened within a few years), Kheel was pleased to be at it again. Although Mayor Michael Bloomberg's plan for an $8 congestion fee to reduce traffic into Manhattan had died in the state legislature, Kheel proposed a far bolder plan: make the New York City subways absolutely free—and pay for it with a $16-per-car congestion fee, twice what the mayor had proposed.

As Kheel sees it, Bloomberg had a good idea but made a fatal error. "The mayor started with a negative: an $8 fee for entering the business district. The majority of people who would have to pay it would be against it. I say, start with a positive—free transportation for everyone—and create a huge constituency in favor of your proposal." Nurture New York's Nature put $100,000 into a study, by the Institute for Rational Urban Mobility, which concluded that the policy would cut congestion by 25 percent and slash greenhouse gas emissions—all for $16 per car, the same price Londoners are now paying to drive into their central city. Kheel says Mayor Bloomberg liked his idea but decided it was politically unfeasible—so Kheel is looking forward to the mayoral election of 2009. "This will be a big issue," he says. "I promise you that."

Which can only mean that Ted Kheel, after all these years, is still ahead of his time. ≈

Chasing Kismet

by JEREMY GERARD

illustrations by APFEL ZET

W HEN ROGER HORCHOW GOT A CALL RECENTLY FROM HIS THEATER
partner asking him to invest in a new musical, the Dallas catalog magnate turned
Broadway producer demurred, but he didn't hang up.

"I asked, 'What's it called?' and he said *Curtains*," Horchow told me. "I said, 'Count
me in.' My first job out of the army was in the curtains department at Foley's, in the
basement. Karma's there."

In the half-century between selling curtains at Foley's, in downtown Houston, Texas,
and selling *Curtains* in Times Square, Horchow has been driven by a singular belief
that his own good taste would resonate with others. His eye for goods earned him millions of dollars as proprietor of the Horchow Collection, the first luxury mail-order

catalog not connected to a bricks-and-mortar establishment, and millions more when he began producing the kind of Broadway shows he'd seen during his undergraduate days in the late 1940s, when new plays and musicals worked out their kinks in New Haven before coming to New York.

At Foley's, the quintessential middlebrow department store for the postwar boom economy, he succeeded by ignoring his own taste.

"If I didn't like it, I would buy it and it would sell," Horchow told me one brilliant June afternoon during a conversation in the light-filled living room of his sprawling North Dallas home. "I sold plastic flowers, tons of 'em, thousands of 'em, plastic dishes, all kinds of stuff." In 1960, after seven years at Foley's, he was recruited by Neiman Marcus, in Dallas, which catered to a far higher stratum of customer. By the time he mailed out his first catalog in 1971, the Collection, with its imported antler chandeliers and high-style serving dishes, was the exact reflection of his taste and his taste alone.

A refined yet highly populist aesthetic is only one clue to Horchow's success. To understand the rest, it helps to visit his home, a rambling white clapboard affair that is surely the most unprepossessing house in J.R. Ewing's neighborhood, about five miles from the steel-and-reflective-glass pin cushion that is downtown Dallas. This is where I found the real Horchow collection, which isn't chic, lacks any exotic provenance, and isn't for sale.

To reach the mother lode of Horchow's 80 years of collecting, you cross the cathedral-ceilinged living room, dappled in sunlight and vibrating with the upbeat primary colors of folk art from around the world, and go through the backyard to a well-appointed studio that resembles nothing so much as the barroom of the "21" Club on steroids. There are toys and gizmos everywhere. Floor to ceiling, it's the Louvre of toys, organized by theme: the transportation theme — buses, planes, cars — the religious theme, the musical instruments theme and the like.

Horchow guides me through it all, past desk and computer, stacks of mail—the usual detritus of the home office—into a small, windowless room, where he reaches down into a dark area and pulls out a single wide, white plastic binder. Opening it, he could be a proud boy rolling out the Torah scrolls on his bar mitzvah day, but what is revealed when Horchow opens the binder is not a holy text. It's his middle school report card.

"Well, look at this," he says, beaming. "All As in seventh grade."

Horchow's collection begins in 1934, when he was six years old, and remains a work in progress. Each of the nearly 60 meticulously assembled volumes has been replicated for his three children, just in case a fire destroys the originals or the Trinity River overruns its banks and oozes up the Dallas North Tollway.

In addition to report cards, the plastic-coated pages hold family photographs, newspaper clippings, theater ticket stubs, menus, programs, love letters, canceled checks, bills of sale, notes for speeches, playbills, a check for $1 million, catalogues, tuition bills, postcards, jottings to himself and others, handmade Father's Day cards, travel directions—treasures and touchstones from a life savored as much as lived.

Indeed, for a man who built his fortune on luxury goods, who owns a pied-à-terre on Fifth Avenue in Manhattan and a summer house on Nantucket, who casually points out the 4,000-year-old Chinese vase in a corner of his living room, who launched a second career as a Broadway producer while practically boasting that he didn't have a clue how to go about doing it, for a man of all these expensive vocations, avocations, obsessions, gambits and desires, for all that, Horchow is a man of surprisingly simple passions.

When most people think of the Horchow Collection, for example, what probably comes to mind is that $8,775 Daum black crystal cheval you've been hankering after, or some similarly eccentric item. But while Horchow prizes such goodies as much as the next impulse buyer, he points out that the three most popular items sold by the Horchow Collection were a $6.95 set of eight glass dessert bowls and saucers, an extendable feather duster and a "hero" helmet for children.

The genius of the Horchow Collection wasn't just pricing, it was the irresistible mix of the exotic and the everyday, side by side, all made available by mail order. All you had to do was pick up the phone and take out that new credit card.

"Half of the Collection was stuff that you could buy anyplace but didn't, and you saw it there and you began to realize how easy it was to get," Horchow says. "And the other half was, we traveled all the time and we had buyers and our rule was you don't have to like it yourself, but you had to have someone you would send it to. Not 'the children's schoolteacher,' but a specific person. It kept us focused."

Of course, it helped that by the time he started the Horchow Collection, he'd been pushed out into the world by mentors with impeccable taste, and that he'd already stretched far beyond his own upper-middle-class American beginnings.

"I was born in Cincinnati, Ohio, where my parents built the first house on their street," Horchow says. His parents sent him off to boarding school and he later matriculated at Yale, his father's alma mater, which he attended on scholarship.

While he was at Yale, Horchow happened to get a pretty good education in the theater, especially the musical theater, which he'd grown up loving ever since George Gershwin himself had played the family piano during a swing through town.

"When I was five-and-a-half, George Gershwin came to Cincinnati and played that piano," he says, pointing to the very piano in his living room. "My mother was a concert pianist, and she played Bach, Chopin, et cetera. Gershwin came to Cincinnati and she went to hear him, then backstage to have him sign a songbook. Knowing that he was leaving on a one o'clock train from the station, which was near our house, she invited him back to our home. That's when I heard him. I was upstairs, and I heard this music that was so different. I came downstairs and it was George Gershwin. I didn't know who he was, but forever after, I loved Gershwin's music. I got hooked on him.

"At Yale, I could walk to the Shubert Theater, which was two blocks from my dormitory, and for two dollars I could see everything," he recalls. "*South Pacific*, *Death of a Salesman*, everything. In my junior year, *South Pacific* was previewing in New Haven, and my date for the junior prom's real boyfriend was the understudy for Ezio Pinza. So we went backstage that weekend, and I met Pinza, Mary Martin, Joshua Logan, Richard Rodgers, all of 'em. I was a kid!"

Though he started out as a small-goods buyer at Foley's, his real education got under way at Neiman's, whose customers depended on the Marcus family to have their fingers on the pulse of fashion and furnishings. It was a mandate that Stanley Marcus and his brother Edward, who ran the business, regarded as a sacred trust.

"Stanley was very concerned about the look of everything." He forced Horchow to analyze every buying decision he made. "He'd come in and say, 'Well, why did you buy this?' And gradually I learned the business," Horchow recalls, his voice an easygoing adenoidal drawl befitting a man comfortable in his own skin. Stanley also taught him an appreciation for upscale interior design that quickly became Horchow's second nature. "He'd create some reason for me to deliver something to somebody's house, and he'd say, 'You go in that house and look around and see what they have,' which I did."

At Neiman Marcus, Horchow started as the china, glass and gift buyer, eventually rising to rule the growing mail-order business. Neiman Marcus had just begun sending out advertisements with their monthly bills and the first glossy Neiman Marcus catalogues began showing up in mailboxes.

Before long, he sensed the world of the consumer was fundamentally changing: You no longer had to have a store to sell merchandise. Horchow saw an opportunity with the Kenton Corporation and jumped at it. Kenton was a consortium that included

Valentino couture, Mark Cross leather goods and Cartier jewelry, among other items. There was, however, no Kenton store. Horchow launched the Kenton Collection catalog, which made its debut in February 1971 (you can check it out right there in that white plastic binder; there's also a framed copy on the wall of Horchow's office). A year-and-a-half later, scraping together $1 million in financing from his doctor, lawyer, friends and family, Horchow managed to buy the catalog — but not the name. He christened his new baby the Horchow Collection.

"Now, it was my money, and I was not afraid to buy things. I had always loved to travel. We traveled all around the world, all the time," Horchow says. "Some of it was social connections. I had two buyers who had a whole network of friends who knew everything chic and new. And when they would come back from Europe, I'd say, 'What did you bring back?'" A cut-glass crystal rose bowl from Scotland became a big seller that way, as did G. Lalo correspondence cards from Paris. Eventually, Horchow bought out his original investors while riding the mail-order wave he had helped create.

But he wasn't through with Neiman Marcus. When he turned 60, Horchow decided to sell the Collection. The best buyer was General Cinema, on behalf of its subsidiary, the Neiman Marcus Group. "It made perfect sense," Horchow says. "I was in Nantucket for the summer, flew to Boston, told them how much I wanted, said it had to be all cash, and it was done."

In 1988, General Cinema paid $117 million for the Horchow Collection.

....

On the second day I spent with Horchow in Dallas, we met at a local bar and grill called the Stoneleigh P. The P stands for Pharmacy, the remnants of which are still evident in the fountain-style seating and the racks of magazines for patrons to thumb through. In a city that prides itself on change, the Stoneleigh P is a throwback, still playing pop music from several decades past, still slow on the uptake where messy tables are concerned, still serving your choice of burgers or burgers for breakfast (there are other offerings but they're an afterthought).

It is not the place one would expect to dine with the founder of the Horchow Collection, and yet, when he shows up, Horchow is greeted like the regular he is; finding solace in the unchanging menu and musical repertoire, he eats here at least once a week.

Even before he sold his business, Horchow says, he began indulging his stage-struck side, and, as always, his touch was golden. He invested $10,000 in a musical version of *Les Miserables*. He became an early backer of British impresario Cameron Mackintosh, and the resulting stakes in *Les Miz* and *The Phantom of the Opera* earned Horchow—and are still earning him—piles of cash.

Once the Collection was sold, Horchow was free to take the next step from business entrepreneur to showman. "I thought it would be wonderful to do a Gershwin play on Broadway, like *Girl Crazy*, because it had such great music," he said. At the time, Mackintosh wasn't interested in revivals. Horchow's family urged him to do it himself.

"I had received all this money, and I thought, *I'll just do that*. I didn't know anything."

His first hurdle was securing the rights, which required a visit to Lenore Gershwin, Ira's widow, in Los Angeles. "She said, 'What do you know about the theater?' I told her my George-played-my-piano story. I pulled out every stop I had," Horchow recalls. When he recounted a long-ago visit to her sister's apartment in New York, Lenore "tested me, and I said, 'And on the stairway there was a portrait, it might have been of you, painted by George Gershwin,' and she swelled up like a toad. She was my new best friend."

To help him negotiate the Broadway territory, Horchow enlisted Elizabeth Williams, an experienced hand who'd been part of the Mackintosh crowd. He had only one rule for the show.

"I said, 'Look, this is a huge amount of money, I want it to be the very, very best it can be. I don't ever want to look back and say, *Oh if only*.... Let's just go for broke.'"

Girl Crazy, renamed *Crazy for You* and somewhat rewritten, opened on February 19, 1992 at the Shubert Theater on Broadway. It won the Tony Award for Best Musical, ran four years, and was an enormous artistic and financial success. It introduced a new generation to the Gershwin catalog with a score that included "Someone to Watch Over Me," "I Got Rhythm," "Embraceable You" and "Nice Work If You Can Get It." Reviewing the show's out-of-town tryout (in Washington, not New Haven), *Variety* had predicted that "this show is going to make a lot of people happy," and *Variety* was right.

Horchow, however, had no intention of staying in the business. But Broadway glamour proved too hard to walk away from.

"I did that play, and I wasn't ever going to do any more," he admits, "but during that time I met Roger and Brook Berlind, and we became very good friends. He called and said he had the rights to *Kiss Me Kate*. I said, 'I'm not doing any more plays.' But then, I have this stupid head for trivia, and I remembered that at Yale, Cole Porter lived in Vanderbilt Hall, where my father lived, the same room, and I thought, *The karma must be there*. I called Roger and said, 'Count me in.'"

The Rogers, as they're known on Broadway, share more than large checkbooks and keen business acumen. They're as crazy for show business as Bobby Child, the tap-dancing hero of that Gershwin musical who takes a New York City taxi to the Nevada desert just for the chance to put on a show.

This past season, the Rogers were among the presenters of a revival of *Gypsy* for no more reason than the conviction that a great star, Patti LuPone, deserved to be seen by the world's most demanding audience in a role she was born to play. For their efforts, LuPone won a Tony Award; the play didn't. *Curtains* also came up short, closing at a loss due to the stagehands' strike during the fall season.

Horchow's mentor in retail, Stanley Marcus, is gone now, but he still looms large in Horchow's life—even in his second career as a Broadway producer. "When I left Neiman Marcus to create the Collection, Stanley told me, 'No one will ever buy from that.' I said, 'Well, I really think it'll work.' And then about two years later, he told everybody, 'I told him it would work.'

"And when I sold the company and went into theater, Stanley called and said, 'I hear you're going to do a play, a musical,' and I said, 'Yes . . . ,' and he said, 'What do you know about musicals?' I said, 'Well, Stanley, I like musicals, and when I was at college I saw a lot of them, 'cause they all opened in New Haven.' 'Well, what makes you think you could produce a musical?' 'I don't know, but I'm going to try, and it's my money.' He said I was throwing it away. But the minute we won the Tonys, he told everyone in town, 'I told him. . . .' By that time, we were quite good friends and I said, 'Stanley, you said it would fail, come on, 'fess up.'" Horchow pauses. "Stanley took great pride in me."

....

Lately, a third line of work has come Horchow's way, just as serendipitously as the previous two.

While vacationing in California, he became friendly with *X-Files* creator and director Chris Carter. Horchow got a taste for performing when he played a father for eight performances of *Crazy for You*. Now, he admits, he's a starstruck ham. He produces some iPhone photographs from his *X-Files* shoot.

"Chris wrote a part for me in the *X-Files: I Want to Believe* sequel," Horchow says, smiling again like the seventh grader who got all As. "I play Elderly Gent. Chris said, 'The bad news is you have to come to northern Canada. In late January.'

"I said, 'I'm there.'" ≈

Fly Girl

by JENNET CONANT

illustrations by HELLOVON

A FIRST LOOK AT THE ELEGANT DOROTHY MEYER, A STRIKINGLY pretty, petite, blue-eyed blonde, would not lead one to think she once spent her days wielding powerful machinery, crawling under the bellies of aircraft, or solving mechanical problems. This glamour girl, with an affinity for pearls and Diane von Furstenberg frocks, seems far better suited for magazine covers than coveralls.

Dorothy, or "Dorky" as she was known growing up, has spent her entire life defying expectations. But it's a life that could have looked very different if at least one person hadn't known well the spirit and smarts that lay behind the well-manicured veneer.

When World War II broke out, Dorothy's oldest brother, an engineer with Grumman, enlisted in the navy. On his way out, he stopped to make one last fateful employee suggestion, telling the boss, "I have a little sister in New York who would be awfully good at this job."

In the wake of Pearl Harbor, the aircraft factory was losing scores of young engineers to the service, and Roy Grumman did not need to be told twice. He founded Grumman's "junior engineer" training program, recruiting as many enterprising little sisters as he could find. A graduate of stenography school, Dorothy, like most young women of her generation, had few options upon entering the workplace and had taken a position as a secretary. With all the boys going off to fight, however, she agreed with her brother that she was wasting her time at the bank and gamely agreed to try her hand at critical war work.

In 1942, Dorothy joined Grumman's training program and spent eight months at Columbia University taking an intensive course in drafting. After successfully completing the course, she and 10 other "lady draftsmen" were sent to the Grumman plant in Bethpage, Long Island, where they were expected to work their way through the whole shop, doing a one-week shift in every section, until they understood the organization from the ground up. Mr. Grumman instructed the heads of all the different departments not to give the women any extra help — they were to be treated just like "one of the guys." Dorothy learned to rivet, to weld and to operate the powerful nibbling machines used to cut through metal, coming home at the end of each day covered head-to-toe in thick, greasy black oil. She tied her hair up in a bandanna, pulled a jumpsuit over her clothes and mastered the nuts and bolts of aircraft production. She was one of the boys, all right, though it did not escape her notice that when it came to a particularly difficult, messy job that involved crawling into the back of the airplane where there was little room to maneuver, it usually fell to her. "It was an education," she recalled, laughing.

Grumman subscribed to Wilbur Wright's philosophy that you had no business building planes if you could not fly them. "If you really wish to learn," Wright had said, "you must mount a machine and become acquainted with its tricks by actual trial." Dorothy took him at his word and, along with half a dozen young male engineers, signed up for flying lessons. She spent her weekends at a small airport in Armonk learning how to taxi, take off, fly and land safely. They stayed in a broken-down board-inghouse with a fussy old lady proprietor who ran a strict establishment and made sure no funny business went on between the flyboys and her solitary female guest.

When Corky Meyer, one of Grumman's top experimental test pilots, first spotted Dorothy, she was working in a drafty section of the plant known as "Siberia." In a sea of khaki overalls, the corner of her purple herringbone skirt caught his eye. When he asked her out on a date, he had no idea what he was getting into. He may have flown all of Grumman's famous cats—Hellcats, Tigercats and Wildcats—but he had absolutely no clue how to handle blue-eyed blondes. The first time he pulled over and went in for a kiss, he wound up getting slapped in the face. Hard. She planted a powerful right-hander on his left cheek and left him in no doubt that he had violated protocol. From then on, he proceeded with caution, but he was in for a few more surprises.

On one of their first dates, Corky apologetically explained that he would need to duck out early to fix his car. He had been cleaning out his fuel pump and accidentally dropped the bowl, and it had shattered upon hitting the ground. He would have no wheels until he hunted down a replacement part. Dorothy just gave him a knowing

look and left the room. She returned a few minutes later with a tray bearing six shot glasses and suggested he pick one. Sure enough, a pot-bellied glass with gold stripes slipped snugly into place, a perfect fit. It was still in the car when he sold it four years later.

Another time, when they were driving to Stowe, Vermont, for a weekend of skiing, steam began pouring from the hood of his car. It was close to midnight, and not a light was to be seen in the small village they were passing through. Corky was at a complete loss as to what to do. "You need to reverse-flush the radiator," Dorothy told him matter-of-factly as he slowed to a stop. She calmly pointed to a garage that was locked up tight for the night and suggested that perhaps the owner might live in the house next door, where a dim light flickered in the window. The next thing he knew, the sleepy garage owner had been rousted from his bed and talked into lending them his tools. With Dorky issuing step-by-step directions, they succeeded in reverse-flushing the radiator and were back on the road in half an hour.

By then, he had already come to the conclusion that he could not get along without her, and on April 7, 1945, Corky and Dorky tied the knot in a modest wartime ceremony, with a phalanx of pilots as their witnesses. Being married to an experimental test pilot is a nerve-racking business, but, because she had worked at the plant, Dorothy had more confidence than the other wives. She knew what the slogan "The Grumman Ironworks" meant and took it to heart every bit as much as her husband. Grumman built fighters for the navy, and the company prided itself in producing planes that could fly through anything—from fierce storms to a hail of bullets—and still bring the boys home in one piece. When the navy wanted to find out how the Wildcat would fly with a damaged wing, it was her husband's task to take the plane up with an explosive charge attached to one wing, detonate it midair and bring it back down again. When the navy wanted to find out how the Wildcat would fly with two damaged wings, they attached two explosive charges, blew both wings off in midair and watched to see whether the wingless cabin could coast onto the Grumman field. The first thing a good test pilot's wife learned was not to ask too many question that began with, "What if?"

After the war, her husband and a number of veteran fliers got together and founded the Society of Experimental Test Pilots. Every September, they would gather in Beverly Hills for meetings and what amounted to a weeklong party. "Well, those were pretty wild parties, let me tell you," recalls Dorothy, shaking her head. "Everyone would come, and we'd all carry on, running around between each other's suites." Many of the Project Mercury and Apollo astronauts—John Glenn, Pete Conrad, Jim Lovell, Alan Shepard, Gus Grissom, Ed White and Roger Chaffee—were former test pilots and close friends. Many of them had served as Corky's chase pilots at one time or another and had hung out at the house. They were just kids during the war, "JGs," or junior-grade lieutenants. Now they were all famous. "They'd all be there, and they were just great guys, the nicest guys in the world," she says wistfully. Grissom, Chaffee and White died in 1967 when their three-man *Apollo 1* command module erupted into flames during final preparations for their space flight.

Dorothy stopped flying planes when she got married. "My husband took that seat," she notes dryly. After the birth of their two sons, Pete and Johnny, "I never stood a chance." Both boys got their pilot's licenses, though only Pete followed in his father's footsteps and made flying his profession. Their youngest, daughter Sandy, chose to keep both feet on the ground. The role of mother and grandmother has not stopped Dorothy from looking for new challenges. Not long ago, she tried parasailing. Nothing to it. ≈

EACH ONE, TEACH ONE

by VERONICA CHAMBERS

illustrations by ANNABEL WRIGHT

WHEN ULYSSES BYAS WAS A BOY GROWING UP IN MACON, GEORGIA, education was his mother's passion, not his own. His mother worked as a domestic for a white family in Macon while she was in elementary school. The family had three daughters, all of them about his mother's age. When all of the girls—black and white—turned 11, the divide between them became painfully clear. The black school went only as far as the sixth grade. As Byas's mother cleaned the white family's home, she cringed as the daughters described all the fun they had in junior high school and, later, high school. The future Mrs. Marie Smith Byas Sharpe vowed, "All of my children are going to graduate from high school."

It was not a vow that was easily kept. Byas could not remember his father ever living with the family, and by the time he was a teenager his mother was a single parent with six children, living on four to six dollars a week. At the age of 14, Byas decided to drop out of high school to help support her. He likes to joke that he returned to school because, after working six days a week as a bike messenger, he'd finally "discovered something I hated more than Latin." But the truth is far less pithy. His mother insisted the children stay in school, but as the next to eldest, Byas was anxious to help her. "Everybody in my world," he remembers wistfully, "was a little bit hungry."

Byas eventually graduated from high school, but he was still light-years from becoming the illustrious educator he is today. Almost every bookworm has a story about his or her love of libraries, the hours they spent reading, and the pleasure and escape they found between two hardcovers. But Ulysses Byas is not your average bookworm. It is true that at 84 years old, he has spent countless hours immersed in books. His home library—a trove that includes hundreds of volumes on elementary and secondary education, history, religion, science, philosophy and African-American literature—is so impressive that he has fielded numerous inquiries from universities eager to house his collection. Ultimately, he decided it should go to Emory University in Atlanta.

But it would take him years to reach the point where he felt engaged enough with books and learning to make them his life's work. His favorite subject in high school was shop, which led to an early career—after a stint in the navy during World War II—as a master carpenter. In pursuit of better opportunities than he could find in Georgia, he traveled to New York in the early spring of 1946. There he discovered that while people were "more polite, they would not give me one of those good jobs that I spent all my money looking for." It's for this reason that, even today, Byas refuses to refer to New York as "the North." He says, "I haven't been to the North, I've been to New York. There's 'down South' and 'up South.' Geography makes no difference in this country when it comes to the issue of black and white."

Disappointed with the lack of opportunity "up South," Byas returned to Georgia. After the War, the G.I. Bill made enrolling in college too appealing an opportunity to resist. Byas matriculated at Fort Valley State College (now university) in 1947. "They paid my tuition and gave me $75 a month to live on," Byas says with a grin. "I was rich!"

Soon he found his true calling. During his sophomore year, Byas began volunteering at an adult education center on campus. He worked with one man who was so profoundly illiterate that Byas spent months helping this student learn to write his name. Byas recalls, "He found me one evening to tell me, 'I went to the bank with my paycheck and put it there on the counter, and the man said, like he always did, put your X here. Well, I wrote my name all over that check!'" Byas says he fell in love with teaching right then.

He followed an undergraduate degree from Fort Valley State with a master's, in 1951, from Teachers College at Columbia and a Ph.D., in 1977, from the University of Massachusetts. In the intervening years, he was briefly a classroom teacher but soon set out on a path to lead other educators. At 29, Byas received his first assignment as a school administrator—principal of Hutcheson Elementary and High School in Douglasville, Georgia.

Recalling that time, he says, "I wanted my schools to be innovative," and also to address the unique needs of his students. At E.E. Butler High School in Gainesville, Georgia, where he was principal from 1957 to 1968, Byas noticed that some seventh and eighth graders were suffering academically because they were chronically late and frequently absent. The reason? They were working part-time jobs in order to eat. Byas formed what was dubbed the Butler High School Patrol. They supplied the kids with uniforms, taught them drills and gave them plenty of tutoring, too. The patrol just happened to meet before the start of school—just in time for breakfast and, coincidence of coincidences, at the dinner hour as well.

"We'd tell them, we're keeping you before and after school. We'll serve you a meal. We had maybe 40 to 50 students who didn't have to work anymore to get food on the table. That reduced absenteeism, plus they learned self-control and took a great deal of pride in what they were doing."

Byas soon earned a national reputation as an educator with the mettle to help lead communities beyond the ugliness of segregation. In 1970, at 46, he became superintendent

"Everything Dr. Byas says comes straight from the heart.

"He tells me, 'Everybody has an excuse. Don't let your excuses stop you from becoming the man you are meant to be.'"

of Macon County Public Schools in Tuskegee, Alabama—and the first African-American to head an integrated county school district in the South.

Conflicts over race had driven a deep wedge in the community—and no one put out the welcome mat for an African-American who happened to be an outsider coming all the way from Atlanta. "A board member called me and said there had been protests over my appointment and that I'd be receiving a telegram asking me to withdraw. Well, I did receive that telegram. And I put it right in my file. I did not interpret this as anti-Ulysses Byas. They didn't even know me."

Byas immediately set about calming racial conflicts, improving teaching, giving run-down schools a facelift and bringing the budget under control. Within a few months, he won over even his most vocal critics. And, as always, he never lost sight of his most important constituents—the students.

His legacy in Tuskegee includes a program he initiated to keep girls who got pregnant from dropping out. With the help of a government grant, he found more than 75 young mothers in the community who had been forced to drop out because they had recently given birth and couldn't manage child care and school. His message to them: *We want you back.* The campus of the largest high school soon had an on-campus day-care facility, and the young moms received transportation to and from school, clothing and medical care—all the services the young women might need to turn the "crisis" of an early pregnancy into a challenge they could overcome. "I was severely criticized by some for seeming to 'condone' teenage pregnancy," Byas recalls. "But the number of students dropping out because of pregnancy fell to almost zero." He took some heat for the program, he says, "but it sent the right message."

"Each one, teach one" is a popular phrase in the African-American community, referring, some say, to the time of slavery, when it was illegal to teach a slave to read or write. With formal schooling out of the question, education was, by nature, grassroots. One slave would learn how to read and write, and then she would teach another. Byas began carving out a unique mission: to educate the educators. So, one might say, in his case, it is more than "Each one, teach one." It is more like "Each one, teach thousands."

In the early 1970s, he was the first president of the National Alliance of Black School Educators, and his library is filled with correspondence of how he spent the 1960s and

1970s campaigning, training, leading and sometimes out-and-out fighting for black men and women to rise to the rank of school principal and superintendent, both "down South" and "up South."

Byas moved up South in the late 1970s to become the superintendent of the Roosevelt, Long Island, school district in New York. He brought with him his student-centered brand of pedagogy. His credo: "It's our responsibility as a public school district to educate all children. Children from two-parent homes, one-parent homes, or those children from homes with no parent at all—children! Come! Dramatic or athletic, studious or lazy, lawful or lawbreaker. It really makes no difference! Come!" He also brought a keen eye for the bottom line. The district was awash in red ink—and Byas, a skilled administrator and also a child of poverty, knew how to stretch a dollar.

All these years later, he graciously sidesteps the racial issues he encountered in the New York City suburbs. "It was a non-issue," he says. But Alan Richard, author of *Summerton's Children*, an upcoming book on *Brown v. Board of Education*, says it's easy to underestimate the barriers Dr. Byas broke. "He was among the first wave of black school leaders after desegregation," says Richards. "That made his hiring in Tuskegee in 1970 both remarkable and rare."

Instead, Byas prefers to focus on the grand awakening among his fellow African-Americans, who were beginning to give voice to a hard-won sense of racial pride. This was a time when black was beautiful, he says, and that only fueled his sense of mission—to raise up all youngsters through education. "Many people believed that we needed to deal with problems unique to the black community. We pushed ahead as administrators because it wasn't something we were going to wait for the white community to help us deal with."

Although he has been retired for 20 years, Byas is still pushing ahead. It is a bright summer day in Georgia when he and his wife, Annamozel, arrive for Sunday service at Holsey Temple Christian Methodist Episcopal, one of four black churches in downtown Macon founded around the turn of the 20th century. Rev. Curtis Russell is only half kidding when he says that Byas runs the place. Russell, who arrived at Holsey Temple a year ago, says, "Some churches you go to, you go to be a pastor. Some churches already have a pastor. Dr. Byas is one of the greatest leaders of Holsey Temple."

This particular Sunday is "Hat Day" at Holsey Temple, and Byas, dressed in a dilapidated cowboy hat, manages to win two of the three awards in the men's category: Ugliest Hat and Most Unusual Hat. The whole congregation bursts out laughing as Byas stands to collect his awards and applause.

On occasion, Byas commands the pulpit for a special part of the service that he calls the "children's message," although it is a sermon that resonates equally with adults. One might think that street-smart teenagers would not relate to an 84-year-old man who addresses them with a mini-sermon called "the children's message." But you'd be wrong. Byas is surrounded by many young congregants, who hug him, confide in him, acknowledge him with a swift and familiar head nod that one imagines they use most often in the halls of their high school.

Akira Foster, a tall and lanky 16-year-old, says that it is easy for her to look to Byas as a mentor. "I've known him since I was a baby. Everything he's done inspires me. I've done history projects on him."

When Byas sees a young man in his early 20s, dressed in a black T-shirt and jeans, he addresses him with all the respect of an equal. "The Lord has something in store for you," he says warmly. "I've admired you since the first moment I saw you."

The young man responds by giving his mentor a soulful hug, his fist pumping gently against the older man's back. "Thanks for your note," he tells Byas.

It turns out that the guy in the black T-shirt is Leonard King, Jr. Like Byas, he is a one-time high school dropout. "He's a really, really good guy," says King. "Every time I see him, we fall deep in conversation. Everything Dr. Byas says comes straight from the heart. He tells me, 'Everybody has an excuse. Don't let your excuses stop you from becoming the man you are meant to be.'"

Although his church community looks to him as a father figure, Byas is also surrounded by his extended family. All three of his daughters — one a Ph.D. candidate — live in the area (his only son, Eric, lives in New York). His grandchildren dote on him. His youngest grandson, Robert, age nine, marvels that the old man can still beat him "at arm wrestling and board games."

Age has not diminished Byas's competitive spirit. All the energy he put into fighting segregation for nearly a half-century has to go somewhere. These days, you're likely to see him at his most ferocious when he's cheering on his beloved Atlanta Falcons. His nephew, Leonard Clark, has season tickets, and the two go to at least one game a year together. Clark laughs because, every year, he and his uncle have the same conversation. Clark asks Byas who he thinks will win the game. Byas, sphinx-like, says, "The winner. Winners win." Clark laughs, "I've known him since I was a little guy. He does not like failure. He always says, 'Whatever you're doing, make sure you're the best.'"

Many thought Byas had scaled the highest summit in education when, 20 years ago, the school board in Roosevelt, New York, decided to rename its Theodore Roosevelt elementary school the Ulysses Byas School. This year, the old structure was torn down and a new, roughly $40 million building is being erected in its place. It's a powerful testament, but the bricks-and-mortar legacy does not sustain him.

Most nights, Byas works until 2 a.m. in his library. His most recent project is a book about his 14 years as a high school principal in two Georgia school systems that has just been accepted by the University of North Carolina Press. *Hello Professor*, co-authored by Vanessa Siddle Walker, will be published in spring 2009.

He may be retired from the public school system, but Byas never tires of his favorite topic—education, and the bounty that comes to those who embrace knowledge. Just recently, he gave his three youngest grandchildren a gift that he believes will benefit them like none other: a leatherbound collection of the "100 great books" of all time. How did the 9-, 14- and 17-year-olds feel about this gift of literature, the largely ancient musings of philosophers, poets and storytellers? "They were ecstatic," Byas says. "They're all real smart and good students."

Mrs. Marie Smith Byas Sharpe would be proud. Denied the opportunity to attend high school in her time, she lived her dream of seeing all her children receive a diploma— and much more. Byas recalls that he had to tell her what a master's degree was when he went to New York to pursue one. She laughed and said, "I used to have to practically call the police to get you to go to school. Now I guess I have to call them to keep you out!" ≈

Imprint

by SUSAN GREGORY THOMAS

illustrations by SEYMOUR CHWAST

"WHAT WE LEARN ONLY THROUGH THE EAR MAKES LESS IMPRESSION
upon our minds than what is presented to the trustworthy eye," observed the Roman
lyric poet Horace. There's a timeless observation if there ever was one. Horace could
only have intuited it, but science now knows that we are wired as visual creatures from
birth. The moment an infant opens his eyes, he is neurologically imprinted by high-
contrast images: his mother's face, pictographs on a mobile, light filtering through the
branches of a tree. Life continues, and he is stamped by the Christian cross, the golden
arches, the peace sign, the interlocking Cs of the Chanel logo, the Stars and Stripes.
And so it goes. Over time, each of us layers such images with meanings assembled from
experiences. But it's the original strike to the retina that makes the first dent. We are all
persistently, literally, branded by our first visual impressions.

The U.S. culture is more arrestingly visual, more brand-identified, than any in the world—more so now than it ever has been in its relatively short history as a nation. Certainly, the wordsmith of the ancient world never could have imagined how ridiculously prescient his observation would be. Perhaps this is, in part, because he never could have imagined America. Moreover, he didn't know Tom Geismar.

Now slightly stooped, an affable man with an open face, Geismar is also, in the estimate of a great many in his field, a trailblazer of modern graphic design. His work has changed the way Americans and much of the world view life—literally. Picture in your mind's eye the enduring logos of the past half-century. Mobil, Xerox, Chase Manhattan Bank? Those are Geismar's. PBS's accordion of profiles? Geismar's design. National Geographic, Rockefeller Center, the Boston T? All Geismar. The list goes on. As chairman of the U.S. Department of Transportation Advisory Committee on transportation signs and symbols in the 1980s, he oversaw development of a new national system of standardized symbols, earning him the Presidential Design Award in 1985. Geismar has designed and curated major exhibitions for national landmarks, including Ellis Island in Manhattan, the Smithsonian's National Museum of American History on the Mall in Washington, D.C., and the Library of Congress.

Don't just be impressed. Be awed. Today, graphic design plays such a deeply intrinsic role in how we see that its presence often escapes our conscious notice. But consider: Just a half-century ago, only a select group of insiders who knew about fashion could identify the chic woman with a knowing appraisal of her handbag and matching shoes. Today, anyone can spot the Louis Vuitton, Gucci or Dior logo emblazoned on her sunglasses or trench coat. When Geismar was a boy, families switched on the radio to listen to their favorite serials; now, we all tune in to the branded networks HBO, Showtime, TBS or PBS. Until a handful of years ago, if a person was thirsty, she would find a water fountain. Now she'll ask for Fiji bottled water.

But it was a different world in the late 1950s, when Geismar launched his career. Back then, few people, even Manhattan cognoscenti, knew what graphic design was. When Geismar was asked at dinner parties what he did for a living, people would give him a polite, mystified look and then turn to the person sitting next to them. He was more than comfortable eating his meals in happy silence. That says a lot about him.

Geismar has always played the foil to his rather more shoot-from-the-hip business partner, Ivan Chermayeff. The two met in the mid-1950s at Yale, where they were both studying typeface design to earn their master of fine arts degree. The London-born Chermayeff was the son of the distinguished architect-teacher Serge Chermayeff; he had attended Harvard and the Institute of Design in Chicago. Geismar was born in a commuter town in New Jersey and had earned joint undergraduate degrees from Brown and the Rhode Island School of Design. Geismar was quiet, contemplative; Chermayeff was gregarious, dashing. It was a perfect match. They set up their firm, Chermayeff & Geismar, in New York in 1957.

If the field of graphic design was pedestrian at that point, cultural life in New York was not. With pop art in fine arts, bebop in jazz and the controversial *West Side Story* in theater, all the major artists of the mid-1950s and early 1960s were probing the complex relationship of art to commercial and urban life. As graphic designers, Geismar and Chermayeff seized the opportunity to probe them directly; their business was to create unified visual identities for institutions. But instead of unraveling various themes, their goal was to distill and condense them into lasting symbols. The designers' first major hit was in 1960, with their logo for Chase Manhattan Bank. Prior to that, the bank had simply used a miniature picture of the U.S. map as its logo. As a newly formed multi-national corporation, Chase was now represented by an abstract symbol conveying disparate parts folding into a unified whole.

It isn't an exaggeration to say that Geismar's design of the Chase octagon marked the genesis of the meta-world of abstract logos that punctuate our everyday life. What's more is that while his work is still at the cutting edge, his approach has remained the same. According to a news release issued by Chermayeff and Geismar in the late 1950s, the designers' approach "operates on the principle that design is a solution to problems, incorporating ideas in relation to the given problem, rather than a stylistic or modish solution." In spite of the past half-century's wild flux of tastes and styles, the firm's philosophy is unchanged, which is virtually miraculous in the trendy, breathless field of graphic design today.

Much of the reason for the firm's steady vision is not just Geismar's creative genius—though it should not pass without comment. Where his longtime business partner,

admittedly, issues ideas and a design within minutes of meeting with a client, Geismar sits back, absorbs and mulls over the entire life of an image. He is famous for working into the night for days—weeks—creating dozens of designs until he is completely sure that he has produced the right one. At the heart of his scrupulous routine lies an obsession with perfecting even the smallest detail. Evoking the literary maneuvers of poet E.E. Cummings, Geismar will make what seem like tiny tweaks to typography that transform an entire message. Think, for example, of the "o" in Mobil. Were it blue, like the rest of the type, it would simply be another letter. By making it red, Geismar converted it into a wheel, a target, kinesis, America. He made it in 1964.

To maintain such a balanced perspective over a 50-year career would seem to require more than just a perfectionist's sensibility. Anything less than an impossibly meditative equanimity would spell burnout. Geismar's got it. Clients marvel at it, and even after all these years of working with him, his business partner still finds it remarkable. "Tom does not talk very much, but when he does, you listen because he has contemplated what he is thinking about in a thorough, convincing way," says Chermayeff. "He is completely trustworthy."

Frustratingly, for those of us who aim for this state on the mountain path to enlightenment, Geismar doesn't work at it. It is simply the way he is. Ask him, for example, to look back on his career and reflect on moments of failure and success, and he is silent. "I know that thinking about the past is something that people often like to do, but I just don't ever really seem to do that," he allows, after pausing for a moment to think. "There is always so much to think about right now." Ask him if he has developed any rules of thumb that guide his process, and Geismar is nonplussed, albeit cheerful. "No, I just listen for a long time," he says. "After I feel that I've collected enough information, then I start designing." What is a logo trying to show, and what is it trying to hide? "Logos are empty vessels," he says thoughtfully. "They are only meaningful if the actions of the institution imbue them with particular meanings."

It's a keen observation—one that could be made about the man himself. In fact, it's one that his middle child, Kathryn, made as a teenager. Back from college one summer, she invited a group of friends to the family home on Long Island, New York. Her mother, Joan, spent the week carting the young women around, taking them on excursions and cooking every meal. Her father listened to their conversations in his attentive, nonjudgmental way and quietly tinkered with projects around the house. At the end of the visit, Kathryn gushed, "Oh, Mother, everyone loved you, but they really thought Daddy was terrific!" They all commented on how humble, kind and open-minded he was. On further consideration of her response (or perhaps backpedaling, after noting her mother's crushed expression), Kathryn mused that it was precisely her father's quiet, unassuming disposition that caused people to attribute such lofty qualities to him. The empty vessel holds whatever you put in it.

Which brings one to the ultimate question, when considering Geismar: Why does the Buddha smile? Only a wife, particularly one of 50 years, could answer that. "Tom is so gentle, so tolerant—everything I'm not!" chuckles Joan Geismar. "I only get mad at him when he doesn't care about making a simple decision about something that we need for the house, like a couch."

Excuse us, but did we hear that right? The father of contemporary graphic design doesn't weigh in on every design element of his home? "Oh, he couldn't care less about the way the house looks," she says. "We've had an 'interim' sofa for 30 years!" Same thing goes for his personal appearance, especially—wait for it—branded apparel. That's right: Geismar hates logos on his clothes. "He's always asked me to unstitch those polo ponies and alligators from his shirts," she says. "He thinks they're superfluous and ostentatious."

Call it ironic, hypocritical or just plain droll, but it is pure Geismar. He simply loves design and the problems that it can solve. He is, if there is such a thing, an unpretentious purist. Recently, the director of the Seattle-based Experience Music Project asked Geismar to loan his collection of vintage Japanese robot action figures for exhibition at the museum. When hordes of techies appeared at the show, Geismar was stunned by how much cultural significance his toys had for fans. "They knew all their names, what they did, what movies they'd been in," Geismar marvels. "I didn't know about any of that. I just liked the way they were designed." Devotees of vintage Japanese robotics subsequently sent him sheaves of data about his collection via e-mail. Was he amused, annoyed, uninterested? Geismar smiles, eyes wide. "Oh no!" he says. "I think it's wonderful!" ≈

The Gambler's Gift

by JESSE KORNBLUTH

illustrations by MICHAEL PARASKEVAS

H E SHINED SHOES. HE BUSED TABLES. AND AT THE END OF THE summer, when he had saved $2,500 for college, his mother did what she'd promised to do and matched every dollar he'd earned. So when Sid Craig set off for his junior year at Cal State, Fresno, he had $5,000 in his pocket.

On the way, he had a better idea: detour to Las Vegas and thicken his bankroll. But, although Craig's father was a professional—"a low-key gambler; he made a living"— the teenager had not yet learned the first law of success in Vegas: "Lose $100 and quit." Instead, he stayed at the tables.

"I was young," he recalls. "I had no idea I could lose everything. Even with a dollar left, I was still thinking, 'I can get it all back.'"

He did lose it all. And he spent the first semester that year sleeping on the floor of a friend's apartment while he worked to pay tuition. Not that he valued school, for he was a "terrible" student. "I had no desire or discipline," he says. "But I was good at business."

Good with people, interested in money, unafraid to take risks — these are the elements of an entrepreneurial character.

The only question for Sid Craig was: What business?

....

A phone call provided the first answer. Sid was now a college senior, working after school at Pep Boys, when the local Arthur Murray dance studio called to offer him a free lesson. He knew that led to a sales pitch, so he declined. But he liked dancing; when he was very young, his mother made sure he could tap. He liked the spotlight; as a kid, he'd appeared in some *Our Gang* comedies. He liked women with flair. And he liked jobs that would allow him to make money without leaving school.

So he took an eight-week class — to become an Arthur Murray instructor.

After Fresno State, he'd considered selling insurance. He was asked to go to New York to be trained as a stockbroker. But he knew the owner of the Arthur Murray franchise had a pool and a Chrysler. "I've always liked material things, so I always had goals," he says. "I saw Arthur Murray as an opportunity."

He saved his money and bought the Arthur Murray franchise in Salt Lake City, simply because it was the first one that was available. There were a few troubled franchises; he scooped them up at bargain prices. Soon, he noticed, "I was making more money than any of my college friends."

Sid married and started a family. Around the time he became Arthur Murray's largest franchisee, he lost interest in dance studios. It wasn't just that he'd been in the dance instruction business for 15 years and was restless for a fresh challenge. Also a factor: He'd noticed former Arthur Murray franchise owners doing very well in the health industry.

....

We may not always exercise as much as we should or eat only the foods that are good for us, but it's now the rare American who doesn't know that the foundation of good health is regular exercise and a sensible diet. Those are eternal truths, and some people lived by them in the 1960s. But few of those people worked in the weight-loss business.

Back then, gimmicks ruled. Lie on a vibrator-enhanced table as your innards were bombarded with wavelets of electrical energy, and somehow you'd get up from your passive "exercise" toned and refreshed. Want to lose weight fast? Stop eating, drink four "special" shakes a day.

A few years before Nike sold its first running shoe, Sid Craig opened a Figure Magic studio. Its gimmick: wrapping the client like a mummy. "Right business, wrong vehicle," Sid concluded. In 1969, he moved on to Gloria Marshall Figure Salons, which offered a more sensible guide to weight loss. That investment would bring him the greatest return of his life.

....

Jenny Guidroz grew up in New Orleans. Her father needed three jobs to support his large family, but what she'd remember was his positive attitude and appetite for hard work. So it was galling to her to have a child and, months later, still find herself carrying 45 extra pounds and feeling sluggish.

The weight was also frightening. Eight of her mother's nine brothers and sisters had been overweight—and all eight of them died before they celebrated their 50th birthdays. Jenny's mother, who had six children and many extra pounds, was also a casualty. "She died when she was only 49 from a stroke," Jenny recalled. "Looking into that

In the fall of 19
Jenny had dinn
dinner — noth
Then Sid aske
personal quest
your husband?"

75, Sid and
er. A business
g new there.
 her a rare
on: "Where is

mirror, seeing her there in myself, made me realize that if I wanted to live to raise my two daughters, I had to watch my weight."

She succeeded the old-fashioned way: regular exercise, smaller portions, no desserts. "I was sure there were a lot of people just like me who want someone to tell them what to do," she has said. "You'd talk to a doctor, and he would just say to eat less. That was the standard reply. Just eat less than you're eating. What really started me off in this business was my own research into what kinds of foods I should be eating."

Along the way, she realized no one was telling women the simple truth that there were no shortcuts to better health and a more attractive silhouette. The only right answer: long-term lifestyle changes. She became an evangelist for the knowledge she'd painfully acquired; a job at a gym quickly led to managing several more.

Then she decided to roll the dice — she opened her own health club, powered it to success, and sold it. With her profits, she hoped to buy a franchise of a smart, better-known program.

Around that time, Sid Craig became a partner in Body Contour Inc., a chain of women's fitness salons doing business as Gloria Marshall Figure Salons. BCI was a success in California; Sid was eager to open a branch in a city where cooking with butter and flour had created weight problems. New Orleans was certainly that place.

Jenny was the first person he interviewed.

"The moment I met her I knew she was a top winner," Sid said. "She lit up a room when she came into it. When she attended a training session, she was far superior to the trainer I had sent in. It was obvious she was a gem, and, besides that, she was very attractive. She had it all."

Jenny liked Sid's energy and his company's no-gimmicks weight-loss program, which promised results with exercise machines. She signed on to launch Gloria Marshall in New Orleans. Again, it was obvious she should be promoted; she was soon supervising the company's southern region. Another success, and Sid asked her to open more salons in Chicago. Jenny had a failing marriage; here was opportunity and a change of scene.

In the fall of 1975, Sid and Jenny had dinner. A *business* dinner—nothing new there. Then Sid asked her a rare personal question: "Where is your husband?"

Jenny said she was getting divorced.

"That's interesting," Sid said. "So am I."

And that was it. Sid's business was expanding, they enjoyed working together; it was the kind of encounter when two people who think they know one another well feel as if they're meeting for the first time. Their 1979 wedding was small—and in Las Vegas.

Opportunity knocked next in the form of opposition. Jenny wanted to preach the gospel of exercise *and* nutrition. Sid's partners didn't see the wisdom of changing a successful formula. Sid and Jenny left, the company was sold, and the Craigs wondered what they'd do until a two-year noncompete clause expired.

But that clause, they realized, only applied to the United States. The Craigs had never been to Australia, but they knew English was spoken there. Did it matter that Sid and Jenny Craig had never been there? That they had children who liked living in California? Or that they'd never field-tested the concept of a weight-loss program that combined personal counseling, nutrition and behavior modification classes, and its own line of food?

"I was 51," Sid says. "I took every penny I had and invested it in our new company."

A gamble?

"A smart gamble. I don't really think of it as a gamble because this is something we were going to create. We weren't early. And I had interviewed the other companies in the field. But I did bet it all."

....

Jenny Craig Weight Loss Centers. It sounded as if a real woman was involved in the business. And this woman had a compelling story to tell: gaining weight during pregnancy, struggling to lose it afterward, getting into the weight-loss business to share what she had learned. Australians responded to Jenny's directness and her message.

Jenny was the name, the face and concept; Sid was the marketer. Their first year abroad was tough, but it ended with an ever-escalating sales curve. Sid could hardly believe their good fortune. "Every morning, I'd read the reports and shake my head," he says. "It was going so well."

Two years and a day after he signed the non-compete clause, Jenny and Sid Craig returned to the United States.

The Craigs chose Los Angeles as the site of their assault on America. First, because it was home. Then because they believed it could support the launch of 12 Jenny Craig centers. And, most of all, because they'd have plenty of competition. Sid and Jenny considered that a plus, for it suggested that Los Angelinos were acutely aware of the need to look and feel good.

Jenny Craig offered clients something the competition didn't—frozen dinners, sold right at the weight-loss center. The combination of sound advice and convenient food was compelling. Centers in Chicago and New Orleans followed. And then the franchising began. By 1991, there were 521 Jenny Craig Centers in the United States and 96 more abroad.

The Craigs took the company public. Was massive wealth as much fun as building the company? Sid wasn't sure. But, as ever, he had some ideas for what to do with the money.

....

Collectors sometimes say there's no purchase as satisfying as their first. Sid Craig thought that was nonsense. Since 1991—and even more, since 2006, when Nestlé bought Jenny Craig—he set out to enjoy family, collecting and philanthropy.

He started with horses. First was Paseana, an Argentine filly with a penchant for winning races. Then, in 1992, Sid turned 60, and Jenny decided to give him something he might never have bought for himself. At his black-tie birthday dinner, lights dimmed and on came a video of Dr Devious, a very promising 2-year-old.

"How much?" Sid wanted to know. And Jenny had to confess that she paid $2.5 million for the horse.

Sid was speechless, but not for long. Three months later, Dr Devious won the Epsom Derby — the English equivalent of the Kentucky Derby — and Sid found himself, in top hat and morning coat, promising the Queen and the Queen Mother the free breeding that is the British custom. The Queen, in turn, presented the Craigs with a memento from her collection: an engraving of a horse winning the Epsom Derby. That horse was, she explained, the great-grandfather of Dr Devious.

Dr Devious went on to reward the Craigs in more worldly ways: He won more than $1.5 million and was sold a few years later for $6 million. Buoyed by Jenny's gift, the Craigs expanded their stable — and bought a 237-acre training facility in Rancho Santa Fe that they named Rancho Paseana, in honor of their first horse.

The Craigs never got to stand in the winner's circle at the Kentucky Derby, but they had an experience almost as meaningful: In 2003, their Candy Ride set a track record in the $1 million Pacific Classic at Del Mar racetrack. "It doesn't get any better than that in your own backyard," Sid said. "I saw that race 5,000 times before it happened. I really visualized winning that race."

Jenny enjoyed living close to their training facility and the local track. And although she was enjoying private life, her children and her grandchildren, she always went all out for opening day at Del Mar. She'd select two outfits, making her final choice based on the weather. And she gave special attention to her new hat, putting it on just as she stepped out of her limousine. Then, she liked to say, she started "handicapping and praying."

But horses were more Sid's thing. That itch was easy to satisfy; honoring Jenny was harder. "What do you give a giver?" Sid asked himself. And he came up with some over-the-top presents for Jenny. A diamond pendant? That was just for starters. The greater gift was one that could be shared for decades: $10 million to the University of San Diego to be used for a sports center, The Jenny Craig Pavilion. And why not?

Sid had already written a $10 million check to Fresno State, which renamed an entire institution—The Sid Craig School of Business—after its once-faltering student.

Giving became a passion for the Craigs. Jenny bought Franklin Delano Roosevelt's 1935 Lincoln for Sid, and that launched him on a collection of one-of-a-kind cars—and the conversion of a garage at his home in Rancho Santa Fe to a private museum.

To tour that museum is an exercise in escalating incredulity. Tom Mix was driving his customized 12-cylinder Phaeton when he crashed the car and died; here it is, fully restored. Here is Hopalong Cassidy's v-16 1933 Duesenberg. Al Capone's armored Cadillac. Dean Martin's Ghia. Frank Sinatra's Cadillac. A never-produced, one-of-a-kind Jaguar, driven just 197 miles. Clark Gable's gull-wing Mercedes. And FDR's Lincoln. A dozen in all—the equivalent of a wine cellar stocked only with Pétrus.

But the Craigs' best collection is the hardest to see: family and friends. Going on a trip alone would be a defeat for them—for decades, they've filled planes and yachts with people they love. Parties? The Craigs were frequent hosts. Phone calls to friends, gifts honoring special occasions? The Craigs were obsessed.

But it's the addresses of their offspring that really tell the story. From their marriages, Sid and Jenny have five children, and all but one live close by. And then there's the pleasure so deep that Sid mentions it almost in a whisper—he pays the school bills for 13 grandchildren.

....

Regrets? He's had so few. "And I don't collect them," he insists.

The San Diego Padres were almost his. But news of the deal was leaked, and almost immediately the speculation began: "Jenny Craig buying the Padres? Will she substitute carrots for peanuts?" Sid backed off. It was, he now believes, for the best. "I didn't know enough about financing then," he says. "I might just have written a check, and that would have hurt me badly."

No baseball team. And then no basketball franchise: The San Antonio Spurs were another miss. "That team's now worth $400 million to $500 million," he says, shaking his head.

But he did get to buy a piece of the Phoenix Suns. There's always a new horse that's promising; watching a 2-year-old train on the ranch's private track tends to make him think of real races, on public tracks. And then there are unexpected acknowledgments. The Horatio Alger Award is given to individuals who demonstrate that humble beginnings are not, in America, an insurmountable barrier to success. "It's never been given to a couple," Sid says proudly, "but in 2007, Jenny and I were honored with it."

And, yes, there's still gambling. Small wagers on horses, just to hone his interest. And larger plays with dice in Las Vegas. Why not cards? "Craps is a total luck game," Sid explains. "It has the lowest percentage against you. For the gambler, it's the best game in Vegas."

Sid studied blackjack for decades—"lessons at the tables, costing a fortune." Why didn't he gravitate to gambling tables that call for skills, methods, counting? "That's a grinding way to play," he says. "I don't have the patience."

Or the time. With the ranch and main home, a beach house, the cars and art and horses and, most of all, his family, his days are busy. And so, even more, are the evenings, generally reserved for Jenny. After all these years, they still swing dance. And, to his surprise and delight, Jenny turned out to be a terrific poker player.

To be married and work together and still be mad about one another—rare, but that's how it is with the Craigs. After almost three decades, Jenny's assessment of her husband couldn't be more glowing: "Sid has the charisma of a Jack Kennedy, the intelligence of an Alan Greenspan and the humor of a Jackie Mason, along with the good looks of a Clark Gable."

Sid would call that a royal flush. ≈

Sid Craig died at home, surrounded by family, on July 21, 2008.

BIOGRAPHIES

NICHOLAS BELTRANTE
On Guard | p. 14

Circa 1998

JUDY BACHRACH

Judy Bachrach is a contributing editor at *Vanity Fair* magazine and the founder of the recently launched online column *thecheckoutline.org*, which gives frank advice to queries from the dying, and their friends and relatives. After graduating from the Columbia University Graduate School of Journalism, she began her writing career as a television critic at the *Baltimore Sun*; within a few years she was hired by the *Washington Post*'s "Style" section, and after that by the (now defunct) *Washington Star*, where she was a political columnist. Bachrach is the author of *Tina and Harry Come to America*, a biography of the one-time legendary editor Tina Brown.

TAVIS COBURN

Tavis Coburn graduated from California's Art Center College of Design. His clients include *Time*, *Rolling Stone*, *GQ*, the NFL, Nike, Lexus, Sony/BMG, Island/Def Jam and Universal Music. Coburn's style is inspired by 1940s comic book art, the Russian avant-garde movement and printed materials from the 1950s and 1960s. Over the years, his work has garnered many accolades, including top honors from the Society of Publication Designers, the Society of Illustrators and *American Illustration*. In 2005, Coburn was featured in the "Fresh" section of *Communication Arts* and was selected by *Print* magazine as one of "20 Breakthrough Talents Under 30." In 2007, he received a gold medal in the "Illustration: Story" category at the SPD Awards.

OSCAR DE TUYA
Welcome Home | p. 26

Circa 1952

CHRIS SMITH

Chris Smith is a contributing editor at *New York Magazine*, where he writes about politics, sports, crime and sometimes all three at the same time. His cover stories have included profiles of Hillary Clinton, Rudy Giuliani and Pedro Martinez, as well as features on the spectacular declines of *Saturday Night Live* and Eliot Spitzer. He has also written for *ESPN the Magazine* and *The New York Times Magazine*. Smith, a graduate of Duke University, lives in Brooklyn with his wife, Lisa, and their children Jack and Lila.

SCOTT JOHNSON

Scott Johnson was born and raised in Milwaukee, Wisconsin. After graduating with a fine arts degree from the University of Wisconsin, Madison, he moved to Chicago. He is represented by Tinlark Gallery in Los Angeles and FLATFILE galleries in Chicago, and his paintings have been exhibited in St. Paul, Miami and London. *New American Paintings* magazine recently published his work in its 2008 Midwest edition, and previously in its 2006 and 2004 Midwest editions.

JERRY LEIBER
Is That All There Is? | p. 36

Circa 1998

DAVID RITZ
David Ritz, a four-time winner of the Ralph J. Gleason Music Book of the Year Award, has collaborated with, among others, Ray Charles, Marvin Gaye, Aretha Franklin, B.B. King, Smokey Robinson and Don Rickles on their biographies. His novels include *Blues Note Under a Green Felt Hat*; his lyrics include *Sexual Healing*. His most recently published book is *Journey of a Thousand Miles*, written with classical pianist Lang Lang. David is currently working with Leiber and Stoller as well as Professor Cornel West on their memoirs.

BRIAN CAIRNS
Brian Cairns' work frequently appears in international design annuals and other illustration and design publications. He has received many accolades for his work, including a Society of Illustrators Gold Medal and numerous Distinctive Merits from the Art Directors Club. He combines an active freelance career with a lecturing post at the Glasgow School of Art. Cairns exhibits in New York, London, Los Angeles and Japan, and his work is included in the BBC Permanent Collection. Clients include Ridley Scott Associates, American Express, Herman Miller, United Airlines, Nike, Warner Brothers and *The New York Times*. Cairns lives in Glasgow, Scotland, with his wife, Elizabeth, and three children.

MILDRED BOND ROXBOROUGH
Take My Hand | p. 46

Circa 1971

SUSAN CHOI
Susan Choi was born in South Bend, Indiana. She studied literature at Yale and writing at Cornell, and worked for several years as a fact-checker for *The New Yorker*. Her first novel, *The Foreign Student*, won the Asian-American Literary Award for fiction, and her second novel, *American Woman*, was a finalist for the 2004 Pulitzer Prize. With David Remnick, she coedited the anthology *Wonderful Town: New York Stories from The New Yorker*, and her nonfiction has appeared in leading publications and anthologies. A recipient of fellowships from the National Endowment for the Arts and the Guggenheim Foundation, she lives in Brooklyn, New York, with her husband, Pete Wells, and their sons.

LAURA CARLIN
Laura Carlin is a graduate of the Royal College of Art in London, England. She works mainly in the medium of drawing and has won several awards during her studies. Her illustrations have been featured in numerous national and international publications, including the *Guardian*, the *Observer*, the *Sunday Telegraph*, the *Independent*, *New Scientist*, *Vogue*, *The New York Times* and *The New Yorker*. Recently, she has done work on advertisements for British Airways, Trebor and Monsoon, and book illustration for the Folio Society and Walker Books. Carlin won First Prize for Newspaper and Magazine Illustration in the 2006 V&A Illustration Awards and is regularly featured in *American Illustration*.

ARMY & SELMA ARCHERD
The Heart of Hollywood | p. 58

Circa 1970s

SHEILA WELLER

Sheila Weller is the author of seven books, three of them *New York Times* bestsellers, and an award-winning journalist who is currently senior contributing editor of *Glamour* and a writer for *Vanity Fair*. Her current book, *Girls Like Us: Carole King, Joni Mitchell, Carly Simon — And The Journey of a Generation* was on *The New York Times* bestseller and extended bestseller lists for eight weeks. Weller has also written the family memoir *Dancing at Ciro's*, an investigative book on the Alex Kelly rapes (*Saint of Circumstance*), the O.J. Simpson saga (the #2 *New York Times* bestselling *Raging Heart*) and the critically lauded *Marrying the Hangman*. She lives in New York City with her husband, history and science author John Kelly.

JOSIE JAMMET

Josie Jammet's work examines and reinterprets photographic works to create new, previously unseen compositions of the images. Specializing in commercial portraiture, Jammet is often called upon to produce modern-day incarnations of famous historical or literary figures. For example, for *The Guardian*, she relied on a written description of Virginia Woolf's complexion to reproduce, in color, a famous black-and-white portrait of the novelist. Regular commissions from *Sight & Sound* magazine have given Josie opportunities to reconstruct icons of the cinema, such as Orson Welles in *Citizen Kane*. Jammet's clients include *Rolling Stone*, Channel 4, Amylin Pharmaceuticals, Nike, the Guthrie Theater, the *Guardian*, the *Sunday Telegraph*, *The New York Times*, *Men's Journal*, Penguin Books and *World Business*.

WILLIAM PUTNAM
The Good Doctor | p. 68

Circa 2006

DENIS HAMILL

Denis Hamill was born in Brooklyn, New York. His first newspaper job was with *Flatbush Life*, a Brooklyn weekly. In 1976, he joined the staff of *The Village Voice,* and in 1977, he won the Meyer Berger Award from Columbia University's School of Journalism for best New York City reporting. Hamill has since worked for *New York Magazine*, the *Los Angeles Herald Examiner*, the *Boston Herald American* and *New York Newsday*. He currently writes a column for the *New York Daily News*. His screenplays include *Turk-182!* and *Critical Condition*. He has written 10 novels, including *Fork in the Road*, to which the film rights were recently sold to Alexander Payne, the Oscar-winning director of *Sideways*. He lives in Queens.

BRETT RYDER

After graduating from Camberwell College of Arts in South London, England, Brett Ryder began his career as an illustrator working mainly in pen, ink and collage. His discovery of the computer as an artist's tool was, in his words, "a revelation," and he now creates most of his artwork by digitally manipulating his collages and drawings. His work appears regularly in the *Guardian*, *Harper's* magazine, the *Daily Telegraph*, the *Los Angeles Times*, *BusinessWeek* and *New Scientist*. His illustrations have also been commissioned by such clients as Dr. Stuart's Herbal Teas, Penguin Books and Vodaphone. Ryder admires graphic designers Milton Glaser and Abram Games and illustrator Gerard Hoffnung. He is also the proud owner of a collection of Ladybird children's books.

MARK SMITH
True Love | p. 84

Circa 2006

JOYCE WADLER
Joyce Wadler, a New York City writer and humorist, is a reporter at *The New York Times*. Her books include the memoir *My Breast: One Woman's Cancer Story*, which *The London Sunday Times* called "the first breast cancer comedy—albeit a black comedy," and *Liaison: The True Story of the M. Butterfly Affair*. She has a terror of helicopters.

RICCARDO VECCHIO
Riccardo Vecchio was born near Milan, Italy. From 1990 to 1993, he studied applied and fine arts at the University of Trier, in Germany, and spent the following year at the European Institute of Design in Milan. In 1994, he was awarded a Fulbright Scholarship to enroll in the masters program at the School of Visual Arts, in New York City. He graduated in 1996, receiving the Paula Rhodes Memorial Award for his thesis project. Since then, Vecchio has been a faculty member in the SVA illustration department. His work has been commissioned for a wide variety of magazines, books and other media in the U.S. and abroad.

GRACE MCFARLAND
The Greatest of Ease | p. 94

Circa 1931

DAVID EVANIER
David Evanier is the author of the recently published novel *The Great Kisser*. He has published seven other books, including *Making the Wiseguys Weep: The Jimmy Roselli Story*, *Roman Candle: The Life of Bobby Darin*, *Red Love* and *The One-Star Jew*. He has written for *The New York Times Magazine*, *New York Magazine*, *The New Republic*, *The Paris Review*, *The New York Times Book Review*, *The Antioch Review*, *Southwest Review*, *Ninth Letter* and scores of other publications. His work has been anthologized in *Best American Short Stories*, and he is a winner of the Aga Khan Fiction Prize. He is a former senior editor of *The Paris Review*.

PIETARI POSTI
Pietari Posti was born in Helsinki, Finland. After graduating in 2005 from Finland's Lahti Polytechnic with a BA in graphic design, Posti moved to Barcelona, Spain, where he started pursuing a career as an illustrator. Posti has exhibited in numerous group shows around the world, including Now Showing—Exploring the Lost "Art" of the Film Poster, at Cosh Gallery, London (2008). Posti's work has been featured in the *3x3 Professional Illustration Annual* (2007), *PRINT Magazine European Design Annual* (2007) and *American Illustration 27*. His work has been published in *The New York Times*, the *Guardian*, *Wired* magazine and *Paste* magazine and has also been featured in advertising and on merchandise such as T-shirts, wallets and furniture.

RICHARD ZAMBONI
Man and Machine | p. 104

Circa 2002

DAVID KOCIENIEWSKI
David Kocieniewski was raised in Buffalo, New York, where he spent the frigid winters of his youth dreaming of a future as a National Hockey League star or Zamboni operator. A reporter for *The New York Times*, he has spent more than 15 years covering law enforcement, politics and terrorism in and around New York. He has also developed stories from the streets into several long-form projects, including coauthoring a book about the 1993 attack on the World Trade Center, and publishing an exposé on corruption in the NYPD, *The Brass Wall*. He lives in Yardley, Pennsylvania, with his two daughters, both avid skaters, who are waiting patiently for him to one day re-create the fabled rink of his boyhood backyard.

CHRIS SILAS NEAL
Chris Silas Neal, an illustrator and designer, was born in Texas and raised in Florida and Colorado. His work has appeared in a variety of magazines and books, and has been recognized by *Communication Arts*, *American Illustration*, AIGA, the Society of Illustrators, the Society of Publication Designers, the Art Directors Club of Denver, *Print* magazine and the Society of News Designers. He exhibits drawings at various galleries across the country. He currently works and lives in Brooklyn, New York, and teaches illustration at Pratt Institute.

ROSE STYRON
Excellent and Fair | p. 114

Circa 1973

COLIN HARRISON
Colin Harrison is a novelist and editor. For 12 years, he worked at *Harper's Magazine*, serving as deputy editor for the last six. Since 2001, he has been vice president and senior editor at Scribner, where he edits both fiction and nonfiction. He is the author of six novels, the most recent of which is *The Finder*, published in 2008 by Farrar, Straus & Giroux. His books have been published in some dozen countries, and his essays have appeared in *The New York Times*, *New York Magazine*, *Vogue*, *Men's Journal* and other publications. He and his wife, writer Kathryn Harrison, live in Brooklyn, New York, with their three children.

RACHEL SALOMON
Rachel Salomon was raised in the mountains of Utah. When she was very young, she spent afternoons with her grandmother, who introduced her to Japanese art, mid-century modern furniture, antiques, illustrated storybooks and books about painters. Later, Salomon competed as a downhill ski racer, traveling throughout the U.S. and internationally. She studied fine art at Brown University and illustration at Art Center College of Design in Pasadena. She lives in Brooklyn, New York.

SAMUEL SCHIMEL
Out of the Sky | p. 124

Circa 1944

JERRY ADLER
A writer and editor at *Newsweek* for almost 30 years, Jerry Adler has written more than 120 cover stories on social trends, science, medicine and other subjects. Two of his articles were ASME National Magazine Awards finalists. His freelance articles have appeared in *The New Yorker*, *Esquire*, *The New Republic*, *Smithsonian* and many other publications, and he has also been reporter and editor for the *New York Daily News*. He is the author of *High Rise: How 1,000 Men and Women Worked Around the Clock for Five Years and Lost $200 Million Building a Skyscraper*, and, with Allan Gerson, *The Price of Terror*, an account of the legal aftermath of the Pan Am 103 bombing. Adler lives in Brooklyn, New York.

GALE ANTOKAL
Gale Antokal works in chalk, graphite, flour and ash to give her pieces an ethereal quality. Antokal is an associate professor at the School of Art and Design at San Jose State University, California. She has received a visual arts fellowship from the National Endowment for the Arts, and her work has recently appeared in *Harper's* magazine. Her work has also appeared in museums and internationally in public and private collections.

MARY LOU CHAPMAN
Called to Serve | p. 138

Circa 2006

JENNIFER BARRETT
Jennifer Barrett is an award-winning journalist who has written for several major publications, including *The New York Times*, *The Wall Street Journal* and *Newsweek*, where she served as a general editor until the summer of 2008. She is coauthor of the personal finance book *The Smart Cookies' Guide to Making More Dough*. Barrett lives in Brooklyn, New York, with her husband, Victor Ozols, and their son, Zachary. She is currently working on her next book.

LAUREN SIMKIN BERKE
Lauren Simkin Berke uses snapshots to create art that is layered with historic and personal meaning. Her work can be seen in galleries across the country, on book covers and in newspapers and magazines including the *Boston Globe*, *The New York Times* and *New York Magazine* and has been awarded recognition by *American Illustration* and A.I.R. Gallery. Berke graduated from Cornell University with a BA in anthropology and from the School of Visual Arts with an MFA in illustration as visual essay.

RALPH BRANCA
High Heat | p. 148

Circa 1948

IRA BERKOW

Ira Berkow, a sports columnist with *The New York Times* for over 25 years, and a Pulitzer Prize winner, is the author of 18 books, including the best seller *Red: A Biography of Red Smith*, the memoirs *To the Hoop* and *Full Swing* and the recent reissue of a collection of columns, *Beyond the Dream: Occasional Heroes of Sports*. His new book, *The Corporal Was a Pitcher: The Courage of Lou Brissie*, will be published in early 2009.

PAUL ROGERS

Paul Rogers, a native of Los Angeles, has won awards from AIGA, the Association of Illustrators (London), the Society of Illustrators (New York), *American Illustration*, *Communication Arts* and Graphis Poster. His clients include the Los Angeles County MTA, *The New York Times*, Pixar Pictures, the Playboy Jazz Festival, the United States Postal Service and Warner Bros. He has created the official posters for the New Orleans Jazz and Heritage Festival and for Super Bowl XXXVII. Rogers has illustrated two books for children: *Jazz ABZ*, by Wynton Marsalis, published by Candlewick Press in 2005 and selected for the 2006 AIGA 50 Books/50 Covers competition, and *Forever Young*, by Bob Dylan, published by Simon & Schuster in fall 2008.

RICHARD GORDON
Monster Love | p. 162

Circa 1950

PETER HERBST

Peter Herbst is a journalist and screenwriter living in Manhattan. He was a founding editor of *Premiere*, the movie magazine, and was its editor-in-chief from 2001 to 2007. He began his career as an editor and writer at the *Boston Phoenix*, became the music editor of *Rolling Stone* in 1977, and served in a variety of editorial posts at *New York Magazine* from 1981 to 1994, the final five months as acting editor-in-chief. He is a member of the board of directors of the Film Society of Lincoln Center.

JOSH COCHRAN

Josh Cochran is an illustrator based in Brooklyn, New York. His drawings have been commissioned by a variety of clients including *The New York Times*, McSweeney's, the Discovery Channel and Pepsi. He has received awards from many publications and organizations, including the Art Directors Club, the Society of Illustrators and *American Illustration*, and was recently featured on the cover of *Communication Arts*. In his spare time, Cochran enjoys working on his silk-screen prints and spending time with his lovely wife, Jenny, and small dog, Porkchop.

MURIEL SIEBERT

Crashing the Boys' Club | p. 172

Circa 2006

LESLIE BENNETTS

Journalist Leslie Bennetts is the author of the best seller *The Feminine Mistake: Are We Giving Up Too Much?*, named one of the best books of 2007 by *The Washington Post*. A prize-winning reporter and currently a contributing editor at *Vanity Fair*, Leslie was previously at *The New York Times*, where she was the first woman to cover a presidential campaign. Her work has been published in *Town & Country*, *New York Magazine*, *Vogue*, *Good Housekeeping*, *Elle*, *Ladies Home Journal*, *The Nation* and *The New York Times Magazine*, among other magazines. Bennetts lives in Manhattan with her husband and their two children.

MICHELE CARLSON

Michele Carlson is an artist, writer and educator whose research investigates the intersection of history and memory, Asian-American studies, transnational adoption, hip-hop and other popular culture. She received both an MFA and an MA in visual and critical studies from the California College of the Arts. Her work has been exhibited in San Francisco at the Patricia Sweetow Gallery, the Giant Robot and the San Francisco Arts Commission, and in Los Angeles at the Cerasoli Gallery, Tinlark Gallery, Junc Gallery and the Korean Cultural Center. Her work is also available for viewing at the Drawing Center's Online Registry Program in New York. Carlson currently lives and works in the San Francisco Bay Area.

KENNETH HEYMAN

View Finder | p. 186

Circa 1968

J.G. DWYER

J.G. Dwyer's writing has appeared in six newspapers, in 18 magazines and under the imprint of nine book publishers. He lives in New York City, which is frequently the subject of his reporting, and has covered wars, national political campaigns, sports championships and playground openings.

PETER JAMES FIELD

British illustrator Peter James Field has a degree in world art history and anthropology, specializing in Japanese culture. He taught for three years at state schools in the mountains of rural Japan. He lives in Brighton, England, and works for a wide range of clients including *Wallpaper* magazine, *Dazed and Confused*, the *Times* and publisher Dorling Kindersley.

THEODORE KHEEL

Artist of Persuasion | p. 196

Circa 1990s

ERIC POOLEY

Eric Pooley, an award-winning writer and editor, is working on a book about the politics of global warming expected to be published by Hyperion in late 2009. Pooley has been editor of *Fortune* and *Time Europe*, and national editor, chief political correspondent and White House correspondent for *Time*. He writes columns about climate change for *Time* and *Slate*. He has received some of journalism's most prestigious awards, including a 2001 National Magazine Award and the 1996 Gerald R. Ford Prize for Excellence in Reporting. He and his wife, Pam, have two daughters and live in North Salem, New York.

MATS GUSTAFSON

Emerging in the late 1970s at a time when fashion illustration was eclipsed in popularity by photography, Mats Gustafson used watercolor and cutout paper works to extend the possibilities of the medium. Today, Gustafson's fashion advertising clients include Hermès, Tiffany & Co., Cartier, Yohji Yamamoto and Comme des Garçons. He has also created portrait and fashion editorial illustrations for French and Italian *Vogue* and *Visionaire*. Gustafson's work has been displayed in publications and exhibitions worldwide.

ROGER HORCHOW

Chasing Kismet | p. 208

Circa 1950

JEREMY GERARD

Jeremy Gerard writes about the performing arts for *Muse*, the cultural news department of *Bloomberg News*, where he is an editor and critic. He has covered American culture as the Broadway reporter for *The New York Times*, as chief theater and television critic and New York editor of *Variety*, and as a senior editor and columnist at *New York Magazine*. Gerard is the author of two books about the theater and has written for *The New York Times Magazine*, *Vanity Fair*, *Esquire*, *GQ* and the *Columbia Journalism Review*, among many other publications. A former president of the New York Drama Critics Circle and chairman of the jury for the Pulitzer Prize in Drama, Gerard lives in New York City.

APFEL ZET

Julia and Roman Bittner and Jarek Sierpinski all studied at the Academy of Fine Arts in Stuttgart, Germany, and started working there under the name Apfel Zet. In 2002, they moved to Berlin to run their first studio. Although none of them had studied illustration, it became the essential element in their work. Apfel Zet like to write and talk about design, architecture and the general failure of Modernism. They love Coney Island, Winsor McCay, Buffalo Bill's Congress of Rough Riders, Elmer Dundy and Frederic Thompson, Chris Ware, Raymond Hood, Edward Hopper and Hugh Ferris.

DOROTHY MEYER

Fly Girl | p. 220

Circa 1960

JENNET CONANT

Award-winning author Jennet Conant began her career as a business reporter at *Newsweek* and later became a contributing editor at *Vanity Fair*. She has written for many national magazines, including *Esquire*, *GQ*, *Rolling Stone* and *The New York Times Magazine*. Her 2002 book *Tuxedo Park: A Wall Street Tycoon and the Secret Palace of Science That Changed the Course of World War II* made *The New York Times* bestseller list. She also wrote the critically acclaimed *109 East Palace: Robert Oppenheimer and the Secret City of Los Alamos* and *The Irregulars: Roald Dahl and the British Spy Ring in Wartime Washington*. She lives in New York City with her husband, *60 Minutes* correspondent Steve Kroft, and their son.

HELLOVON

London-based illustrator Hellovon is heavily influenced by the world of music, fashion and design, and his work blends both traditional and digital mark-making techniques. Since establishing his studio in early 2006, Hellovon has had work exhibited in such venues as the London Design Museum and has had solo shows in Paris, London and New York. He has also built a client list that includes 4AD, Ogilvy & Mather, Non-Format, *Dazed & Confused*, *Wallpaper*, *The New York Times* and the *Guardian*.

ULYSSES BYAS

Each One, Teach One | p. 228

Circa 2007

VERONICA CHAMBERS

Veronica Chambers is the author of the critically acclaimed memoir *Mama's Girl*. Her other books include *Kickboxing Geishas: How Japanese Women Are Changing Their Nation* and *The Joy of Doing Things Badly: A Girl's Guide to Love, Life and Foolish Bravery*. She has also written six books for children, most recently *Celia Cruz, Queen of Salsa*. Veronica has written and edited for national magazines, including *Premiere*, *The New York Times Magazine* and *Newsweek*. She has received several awards, such as the Hodder fellowship for emerging novelists at Princeton University and a National Endowment for the Arts fiction award. She was born in Panama and grew up in Brooklyn. She is married to Jason Clampet, an architecture and travel writer.

ANNABEL WRIGHT

Artist, illustrator and singer/songwriter/guitarist Annabel Wright works from a room in her house in Glasgow, Scotland, her desk an old dining table standing on wooden blocks that are tiered so she can adjust the angle. Wright's clients include Amnesty International, Sony Music, *The New Yorker*, the School of Visual Arts (NYC), Oxford University Press, the U.K. Department for International Development, *The New York Times*, *Food & Wine*, *New York Magazine* and Penguin Books.

TOM GEISMAR

Imprint | p. 240

Circa 2008

SUSAN GREGORY THOMAS

Susan Gregory Thomas is an investigative reporter and broadcaster. Formerly a senior editor at *U.S. News & World Report* and cohost of public television's *Digital Duo*, she has also written for *Time*, *The Washington Post*, *Glamour* and elsewhere. She has two children, ages five and seven. She is the author of *Buy Buy Baby: How Consumer Culture Manipulates Parents and Harms Young Minds* (2007) and is currently at work on a book about Generation X and divorce.

SEYMOUR CHWAST

As director of The Pushpin Group, Seymour Chwast takes graphic styles and transforms them into a contemporary vocabulary. His designs and illustrations have been used in advertising, animated films and editorial, corporate and environmental graphics. He has created more than 100 posters and has written or illustrated over 30 children's books. His posters are in the collections of museums around the globe. Chwast is an American Institute of Graphic Arts gold medalist and is in the Art Directors Hall of Fame.

SID CRAIG

The Gambler's Gift | p. 248

Circa 2000

JESSE KORNBLUTH

Jesse Kornbluth is a New York–based writer and editor. From 1997 to 2002, he was editorial director of America Online. He currently edits *HeadButler.com*, a cultural concierge site he created in 2004. He has been a contributing editor for *Vanity Fair*, *New York Magazine*, *Architectural Digest* and *Departures*, and a contributor to *The New Yorker*, *The New York Times* and other publications. His books include *Airborne: The Triumph and Struggle of Michael Jordan*; *Highly Confident: The Crime and Punishment of Michael Milken*; *Pre-Pop Warhol*; and *The Other Guy Blinked* (with Roger Enrico). He has written screenplays for Robert DeNiro, Paul Newman, ABC, PBS and others, and, for a decade, taught screenwriting at New York University's Tisch School of the Arts.

MICHAEL PARASKEVAS

Michael Paraskevas has had his work featured in *Sports Illustrated*, *Time*, *Town & Country* and *Esquire*, and has earned numerous industry awards. With his mother, Betty, he has published many children's books, including *Junior Kroll*, *Shamlanders* and *Tangerine Bear*, which was adapted for television by ABC. The team developed the award-winning *Maggie and the Ferocious Beast* for Nick Jr. Currently, Michael and Betty are writing and producing the online puppet show *The Cheap Soup*. Their comic strip, *The Green Monkeys*, can be seen at *www.thegreenmonkeys.com*. The two also run the Paraskevas Gallery in Westhampton Beach, New York. Michael was educated at the School of Visual Arts in New York, where he also received a master's degree in visual journalism.

SUSAN ORLEAN • FOREWORD

Best-selling author Susan Orlean has profiled the well-known (Bill Blass, Tonya Harding) and the less well-known (surfer girls, clowns, origami masters), and written "Reporter at Large" and "Talk of the Town" pieces as a staff writer for *The New Yorker*. Prior to that, she was a contributing editor at *Rolling Stone* and *Vogue*. Her best-selling novel, *The Orchid Thief*, about orchid poachers in Florida, was made into the movie *Adaptation*. Her other books include *My Kind of Place: Travel Stories from a Woman Who's Been Everywhere*; *The Bullfighter Checks Her Makeup: My Encounters with Ordinary People*; *Saturday Night*; *Red Sox and Bluefish*; and *Lazy Little Loafers*.

Susan lives in upstate New York with her husband and son.

PEG TYRE · MANAGING EDITOR

Peg Tyre is an award-winning journalist and the author of the best-selling book *The Trouble With Boys: A Surprising Report Card on Our Sons, Their Problems at School and What Parents & Educators Must Do.*

She was a staff writer for *Newsweek* specializing in education and social trends, and has also written for *New York Magazine* and *New York Newsday.* She has taught at the Columbia University Graduate School of Journalism, lectured at Harvard University and speaks frequently to education groups across the country.

Peg lives in Brooklyn, New York, with her husband, novelist Peter Blauner, and their two sons.

ACKNOWLEDGMENTS

With special thanks to the following people, whose hard work, creative spirit and dedication made this book possible: Cynthia Aquila, Michael Braley, Maryann DeTrizio, Ann Dykman, Molly Faust, Alberta Jarane, John Lallo, Jennifer Lee, Patricia Locke, Lindsey Maino, Hans Neubert, Kristin Roth, Lorenz Skeeter and Frank Vaccaro.